PUSHING THE ENVELOPE

By Harvey Mackay

Swim with the Sharks Without Being Eaten Alive

Beware the Naked Man Who Offers You His Shirt

Sharkproof

Dig Your Well Before You're Thirsty

Pushing the Envelope: All the Way to the Top

PUSHING THE ENVELOPE

All the Way to the Top

HARVEY MACKAY

BALLANTINE BOOKS • NEW YORK

A Ballantine Book
The Ballantine Publishing Group

Copyright © 1999 by Harvey Mackay

http://www.randomhouse.com/BB/

LIBRARY OF CONGRESS CATALOGING-IN-PUBLICATION DATA
Mackay, Harvey.
    Pushing the envelope : all the way to the top / Harvey Mackay.
    p.   cm.
  ISBN 0-345-43295-9 (alk. paper)
  1. Industrial management.   2. Creative ability in business.
3. Individualism.   I. Title.
HD31.M238   1999
650.1—dc21   98-45526
                                                                  CIP

Text design by Holly Johnson

Manufactured in the United States of America

First Edition: January 1999

10   9   8   7   6   5   4   3   2   1

DEDICATION

This book is dedicated to all the employees of Mackay Envelope Corporation who for 40 years have turned themselves upside down and inside out to make our customers happy, who have understood from the beginning that the quality of our reputation hinged on the quality of our people, and who have taken immeasurable pride in manufacturing something as simple, and as elegant, as an envelope.

Thank you for pushing the envelope, and pushing me, every single day.

CONTENTS

THE CUTTING EDGE

AVOID THESE OR IT'S RETURN TO SENDER

SECTION TWO: LICKING THE COMPETITION

WHAT EVERY GOOD STAMP COLLECTOR KNOWS

WITH THE RIGHT SPIN, A TWO-CENT STAMP
   CAN BE WORTH MILLIONS

SECTION THREE: HOW I PUSHED THE ENVELOPE

SIGNED, SEALED, AND DELIVERED

SECTION FOUR: THE FLAP ON MANAGEMENT

FROM THE MAIL ROOM UP

CONTENTS

ACKNOWLEDGMENTS

First, and I do mean first, my profound thanks to my executive assistant, Greg Bailey, who is more than an extra right hand. Throughout the writing of *Pushing The Envelope*, Greg was on hand mornings, nights and weekends. And a special thanks to his patient family, too. Greg's skill in coordinating my schedule and my life makes it all possible.

Margie Resnick Blickman is my first set of eyes (after mine) and she has the fastest blue pencil in the west. A great asset to me as my editor . . . even more as my sister.

Lynne Lancaster started out as my speech coach and now she is coaching me on everything. She is the kind of consultant everyone would like to have, and I'm so glad we've been able to work together all these years.

Ron Beyma's range of experience and perception is nearly unparalleled. He's always got something to say and his knowledge has been invaluable to me on all my books.

Scott Mitchell is the president of my company, Mackay Envelope Corporation. I guess you must be able to figure out how good he is and how much I depend on him if I can find the time to write this and other books. He is the leader of my kitchen cabinet, and I always take his advice.

Neil Naftalin has always been able to read between the lines . . . a talent that had paid off for both of us over the years. He's been indispensable to me.

Vickie Abrahamson is a really good friend, the co-publisher

of a top-notch trend newsletter, and one of those people who can make a shiny apple a little brighter. I like to think of her as "Ideas, Inc."

This is my fifth book . . . each one represented by my agent and close friend, Jonathon Lazear of The Lazear Agency. He is the best. And a snappy dresser, too.

Christi Cardenas, Jonathon Lazear's associate, has always been on the ball, and I thank her.

Judy Olausen's photographs hang in some of the best museums, homes, and corporate offices in the world. With good reason. She can even make *me* look good.

Thom Sandberg of Kenyon Consortium designed the cover. The title I gave the book baffled me in terms of how we could convey the idea. But it didn't bother Thom—He went right to it and designed what I believe is one of the better jackets around.

Ken Blanchard is a household name. But in my household, I'm proud to say he's also known as a close friend. Thanks to you, Ken, for all your inspiration.

Rabbi Joseph Edelheit—a man of enormous integrity—was kind enough to read each draft and give me his thoughts. Many thanks to him.

Francie Paper is one of the quickest wits anywhere—she's candid, smart as a whip, and when you ask her opinion, you really get it. But it's always valuable, pithy, and to the point.

Rick Frischman and David Hahn of Planned Television Arts are the best public relations people around. They're not cheap, but as the saying goes, "you get what you pay for."

Leona Nevler, senior vice president of Ballantine Publishing Group, is my editor, but has been my friend since she published my first book, *Swim with the Sharks* in paperback. She always comes through when I need her.

Kim Hovey, publicity director of The Ballantine Books Group, is a real pro. We go way back to other successes.

Lisa Queen, vice president of William Morrow, my first publisher *(Swim with the Sharks)* has become a trusted friend. I thank her for her wisdom, given unselfishly, by reading each successive book and giving me her feedback. Note to her boss at William Morrow: She did this on her own time.

Although editorial enhancement and other changes have been made in terms of contour in the pieces within, grateful acknowledgment is made to United Feature Syndicate which distributes my columns to various newspapers.

Jim Ryan, president of Carlson Marketing Group, is not only a marketing genius, but he helped me decide what belonged on the cutting room floor.

Lloyd Sigel of Lloyds Food Products is my retail guru and always keeps me honest when writing about the industry.

Mary Anne Bailey provided a sharp eye while reading *Pushing the Envelope* in its various stages. Many thanks to her.

Linda Ferraro, my loyal and trustworthy secretary, has put up with me at Mackay Envelope through five books. My thanks for her dedication, good nature, and great disposition.

And finally, ever since I said "I do" back in 1960, my wife, Carol Ann, has continued to astonish me with her knowledge, creativity, vision, resourcefulness, and blockbuster ideas. I still can't believe how fortunate I've been these past 38 years.

How lucky can one guy get?

AUTHOR'S NOTE

Because I write anecdotally, and utilize real-life situations in all of my work, I feel that using gender-specific language lends authenticity to each chapter. Obviously, the message in each of these pieces is not aimed solely at a male or female reader. Have fun with what I'm offering here—and learn from the experiences of both genders along the way.

INTRODUCTION

When you're pushing the envelope, you're looking to maximize your advantage. You're looking for the edge . . . the angle . . . the window.

It's there.

Every business has its tricks of the trade.

It's well known that casinos don't have windows or clocks because casino operators don't want their customers to have distractions or to keep track of time. The fewer the distractions, the longer the player plays, the greater the opportunity for the casino's vig to grind the player down.

It's also common knowledge that hotels have full-length mirrors near the elevators so the guests can admire themselves—and not notice the wait caused by the lack of elevators. Mirrors are cheaper than elevators. That's the hotel's edge.

Some tricks of the trade are not as widely known, maybe because they're not called tricks of the trade.

Religious congregations are notorious for their divisiveness and factions. Smart ministers survive the intrigues and remain popular by creating loyalty through the mundane process of hospital visitations, not fiery sermons. It's called "church building."

Steve Ross, former chairman of Time Warner, was a world-class negotiator who cultivated a surface image of enormous generosity that concealed a powerful inner drive for advantage, control, and wealth. A free charter-plane run to fetch your doggie? The chance to meet a famous movie star? Fun, fun, fun for you. Mon, mon, mon for him.

Even high tech, the engine of America's economic supremacy, is often marketed on a false promise of speed for its own sake.

And there is, of course, my favorite trick of all, the envelope trick. Maybe I like it so much because I'm in the envelope business, and because you can't do it with a fax or e-mail. Or maybe it's because it uses up four envelopes.

Ever since I was a college kid bouncing around Europe with my buddies, I've been on the road, picking my way through different countries, different cultures, different kinds of people and ways of doing business.

That's a lot of bouncing and picking. About thirty-five years of roadwork.

Okay, about forty-five years!

In the process I've learned some of the secrets of the temple. Some are not so secret. They are the homespun lessons of the road: Stay alert. Read the map. Both hands on the wheel. Some are cautionary flags, signs of danger ahead, rough roads, hazardous conditions, dangerous curves. Some are just plain red lights. Stop. Go no further.

When you've done as much windshield time as I have, you've seen almost all of it.

So let's get packed (there's a chapter on that) and get the show on the road (and on that, too).

Section One

HOW TO BE A #10

Chapter 1

MAY I HAVE THE ENVELOPE PLEASE?

I get all my best lines from the movies, which is where I learned to quote Michael Corleone, supposedly quoting Machiavelli, saying "Hold your friends close and your enemies closer."

Rat-a-tat-tat.

Well, my enemies—those low-rent hounds who are always underbidding me—must have seen the same movie, because they are wise to my ways. I try to buddy up to them at all the envelope conventions, but they aren't having any.

How can you rat-a-tat-tat them if they always keep their distance?

So, I make it my business to concentrate on the first part of Michael's homily, and stay close, very close, to my friends.

When Ingemar Johansson fought Floyd Patterson for the heavyweight title in New York four thousand years ago, I was still wet behind the ears and the only guy at ringside without a six-dollar cigar in my mouth and a blonde on my arm. My guest was a machine supplier, so I could be the first kid on my block to get my hands on his new high-speed envelope machine.

I also took care of my buyers. I entertained. I gifted. I schmoozed. I laughed in all the right places.

There are lots of reasons why. When the buyer likes you:

- If you mess up, and I do occasionally, as do we all, you

have a deposit of goodwill to draw against. You will get a second chance.

• When your buyer's company has some big new policy change, the buyer will try to find some way to keep on doing business with you even though he has to cover his backside to show conformity to the big new policy change.

Here's what happened to me at a Fortune 500 company in Minneapolis some years ago. If it happens to you, you might consider employing the fabled "envelope trick."

The policy change: Cut costs. Slash prices. Squeeze those greedy vendors till their stony little hearts bleed and their squeaky little voices cry out for mercy.

The directive to the buyer: All paper, packaging, and printing contracts had to be bid out. No renewing of any contracts whatsoever. Freeze 'em. Tweeze 'em. Tease 'em. Squeeze, squeeze, squeeze 'em.

There were four bidders. I had had the business for 10 years. Ed, the buyer, and I were friends.

And, being the sole supplier every year, I had made it a point to know everyone up and down the ladder, from the vice president of purchasing to secretaries to mail room personnel. I was Good Old Harvey, spreading good old goodwill and cheer to one and all.

So, not having put all my eggs in the buyer's basket, I had a network throughout the company. I worked it to find out who the other three bidders were.

This helped.

I was able to make some very constructive suggestions on how the specs should be drawn up.

This also helped.

Keep in mind, there were still limits. Even though the buyer wanted me to wind up with the business, this had to be an arm's-length transaction. My competitors were no fools. Any hint of collusion and they would cry foul. And they, too, had their pals within the organization.

There were eyes everywhere to see to it that the big new policy change was observed.

Rule: There would be no second looks.

Rule: No chance to change my price.

Rule: No seeing the competition's bids.

Ed was not about to jeopardize his job for me. I didn't expect him to. But he gave me one edge, a very big one. I was to be the last bidder in.

I prepared four envelopes. Each contained a bid:

A. A down and dirty bid, leaving the gunnels of the good ship Mackay about one-fourth of one inch above the waterline. If I had underestimated my costs by one extra pot of glue, I'd be sunk. I prayed I would not have to use it.

B. A modest down and dirty bid, about three inches above the waterline. A couple of good waves would swamp me, but at least I could make it to shore on calm seas.

C. The same price as last year's contract with no price increase. Business as usual.

D. A 6 percent increase, which reflected two paper-price increases in the past 12 months. The America's Cup winner. This was still a fair price, given the boost in the cost of my raw materials, and the buyer would have given it to me if he had not had to get four bidders, but . . .

As we in the bidness world all know, competitors have this nasty habit of trying to buy their way into a new big account one year and worry about keeping it the next. So I was a realist. There was a good chance one of those three bums would underbid me.

So, now I am armed with four bids, not knowing which one I will play. I put bid A in the top of my briefcase, bid B in the bottom of my briefcase, bid C in the left inside pocket of my suit coat, bid D in the right outside pocket of my suit coat.

Time for my summit meeting with Ed. My goal, of course, is information.

We reminisced about 10 years together, years of fun and fellowship, service and self-sacrifice. . . . How in the early days, before I could afford a truck, I used to put his envelopes in the trunk of my car and deliver them to him personally. How we opened the plant on Saturdays and Sundays to fill his orders. How we waived overtime charges when his budget was tight.

Keep in mind, that as I do this jolly reprise, I am running a CAT scan over every inch of Ed. My main focus is to try and read his tone of voice and his body language to detect any hint as to whether, and how much, the competition has chopped me up.

Though Ed knows exactly what I'm up to, Ed is his usual warm friendly self. Nothing has changed in his manner. No better. No worse. NOTHING HAS CHANGED.

In Ed's mind, he is not helping me that much, just schmoozing and batting the ball around. Ed discloses kind of harmlessly that the competitors aren't including the paper price increase in their bids, but on the other hand, didn't attempt to slash their way in either.

So now I know that there will be no price increase. D is dead in the water. Even though my competitors were hit with the same exact paper price increase I was, they decided to eat it in hopes of underbidding me. I know which bid to submit. It's C. I reach for my left inside pocket and turn in my bid. I get the order. Ed's integrity is intact. So is my account.

Someday maybe I'll be skillful enough to apply the second half of Michael Corleone's aphorism about keeping close to your enemies. But in the meantime, I'm going to continue to concentrate on staying as close as I can to my friends. They sure can help you if they want to.

> ### MACKAY'S MORAL:
>
> The reason you always dance with the one
> who brung you, is 'cause when the party's over,
> you may need a ride home.

YOUR GOALS,
EXPRESSLY DELIVERED

Chapter 2

NOW THAT IT'S FEBRUARY, HAPPY NEW YEAR

If you ask the attendant at your health club what the busiest day of the year is, he'll tell you it's the day after New Year's. That's when all the New Year's–resolution types pour in. By February only a handful are left. Now that New Year's Day is well over, tell me, how many of those resolutions have you kept? How many can you even remember?

Maybe you could use a new set. This time, you won't have to fight the crowds.

1. I will improve my listening skills.

I will remind myself that I can't learn anything when I'm doing the talking. I will abandon my phony "open door" policy and establish specific meetings and set aside specific times so that others can have real access to me. I will break down barriers. I will try to end the "not invented here" syndrome and encourage the free flow of information across departmental and hierarchical lines. I will answer my own phone . . . well, I will answer it more often.

2. I will improve my professional skills.

I will cease to be a pothole on the information highway. I will not allow myself to become one of these old fuddy-duddies who brag about their inability to operate modern business equipment. I will get up to speed in computers and communications equipment. Nobody should come into the twenty-first century without being computer literate.

3. I will improve my reading skills.

Unfortunately, my reading ability has slowed down over the years and it is taking me longer to absorb less. I will take a speed-reading course. Instead of reading what merely confirms my existing prejudices, I will search out material that introduces me to new ideas and new ways of thinking.

4. I will waste less time.

I will use my commuter time to read more or to listen to audio tapes that can help me improve my skills and broaden my understanding.

5. I will exercise regularly.

I will do so to the point where I become "positively addicted." I know exercise not only improves my health but helps me maintain a high level of performance on the job.

6. I will encourage risk taking.

I know that many businesses fail from lack of boldness rather than from trying something new. I will not punish or ridicule honest mistakes. I love my work. I want others to feel the same about theirs, so I will try to make my workplace fun and exciting, not just a paycheck.

7. I will put into practice a plan to become the sole source of supply to my largest customers.

The most important element of my plan is to treat my customers as though I were their most dedicated employee and consultant, ready to serve them in every way, so they feel my company is practically a division of their company.

8. I will be committed to growing and improving every facet of our business.

I want every employee in my company to know we are open for hire eight days a week, 13 months a year. I want them constantly to be on the lookout for good people to become part of our team.

9. I will contribute to my community.

I will be a giver. I will give money. I will give time. I will try to make a difference. I want to help make the place I live become a better place for everyone.

10. I will not neglect my family in pursuit of the almighty dollar.

I will never forget that they do more to keep me on an even keel and bring more genuine happiness into my life than any business success I can ever achieve. So Carol Ann, David and Virginia, Mimi and Larry, Jojo and Michael, make room for me. I'm on my way home.

MACKAY'S MORAL:

Start your new year today. And remember, anyone can make a resolution. Very few people can keep one.

Chapter 3

AND I THOUGHT SELLING ENVELOPES WAS TOUGH

There were only two times in my life when I wanted to be older. When I was 15 and the minimum age for a driver's license was 16. And when I was 59 and a marathoner, I knew the next year I'd be ranked against 60 to 64-year-olds instead of 55 to 59-year-olds.

I ran in the 100th Boston Marathon in 1996. By mile 10, I didn't think I was going to get even a minute older. It was my tenth marathon and the toughest. With one mile to go, I hooked up with an old friend, Hal Higdon, editor of *Runners' World*. He was just about to complete his 100th (and this is not a typo, folks) marathon. One hundredth Boston and his own personal 100th. He was grimacing and not looking too good, so I hollered out, "What's wrong? . . . You should be on cloud nine. . . . They can't take this away from us!"

He said he had fallen apart at mile 10, a point at which, for the running elite, the real race hasn't even started. For the last 15 miles, he was just gutting it out.

Twenty-five yards from the finish line, I had to slow down and take in the whole scene. My running partner, Bill Wenmark, had taken out his camera so he could take a picture as I crossed the finish line.

At that moment, Higdon, who by now was five to 10 runners ahead of me, turned back, cupped his hands, and said, "Harvey, that will teach you to stop for a picture."

Hal Higdon's competitive juices were still flowing down to the last nanosecond. The truth is, except for the elite, marathoners do not really compete against each other.

When you are running with 38,000 other people, how can it matter if you finish 8,651st, 18,651st, or 28,651st?

What matters is, you finish . . . period.

There is only one thing runners really compete against— the little voice that grows louder at every split that says: "Stop."

It is, unfortunately, a familiar sound. We hear it all our lives, at work, at school, in our personal relations.

It tells us we cannot succeed.

We cannot finish.

The boss expects too much.

The company is too demanding.

The homework assignment takes too long.

Our family is too unappreciative.

The truth is that many successful people are no more talented than unsuccessful people.

The difference between them lies in the old axiom that successful people do those things that unsuccessful people don't *like* to do.

Successful people have the determination, the will, the focus, the drive to complete the tough jobs.

Why run 26 miles 385 yards?

Why torture yourself to achieve a goal with no tangible reward or significance other than what you yourself assign to it?

The answer lies in the question: Because only you can know what it means, only you are able to make yourself do it.

When you do, then you know there isn't anything you can't *do.*

No amount of hype, no cheering section, no personal glory, no place in the annals of history, can carry you all those miles.

You have to do it yourself.

Your chances of success in life are probably just as good as anyone else's.

Don't shortchange yourself through fear or a preconceived notion that the cards are stacked against you.

At the Boston Marathon, Heartbreak Hill is at mile 18. There are mile 18s in everyone's life.

Some come earlier in the race. Some later.

But wherever you find them, you can overcome them.

Running a marathon is not about winning the race against 38,000 other runners. It's about winning the race against yourself.

MACKAY'S MORAL:

You'll never turn *try* into *triumph* . . . without adding the umph!

Chapter 4

DETERMINATION TURNS THE ORDINARY INTO EXTRAORDINARY

I remember when I was first starting out and asking a colleague I respected how many calls he would make on a prospect before giving up. He told me: "It depends on which one of us dies first."

Determination is what keeps us hammering away. Determined people possess the stamina and courage to pursue their ambitions despite criticism, ridicule, or unfavorable circumstances. In fact, discouragement usually spurs us on to greater things.

Consider Sylvester Stallone and his phenomenal success. As a child, Stallone was frequently beaten by his father and told he had no brains. He grew up lonely and confused. He was in and out of various schools. An advisor at Drexel University told him that, based on aptitude testing, he should pursue a career as an elevator repair person.

He decided to pursue acting, but his abnormal life led to one failure after another. He remained determined to learn his chosen craft and used his failure to try his hand at writing. After watching Muhammad Ali fight Chuck Wepner, a relatively unknown fighter who went the distance against the champion, Stallone was inspired to write the script for *Rocky*—in less than four days.

As Vince Lombardi said, "It's not whether you get knocked down. It's whether you get up again." Five *Rocky*s later, Stallone is a champion . . . of determination.

General Ulysses S. Grant was so determined, like many military heroes before and after him, that he was deemed indispensable in President Lincoln's eyes. After Grant's defeat at Shiloh, nearly every newspaper in the United States demanded his removal. Lincoln's friends pleaded with him to give the command to someone else. But Lincoln said, "I can't spare this man. He fights. He's got the grip of a bulldog, and when he gets his teeth in, nothing can shake him off."

Look at Mother Teresa. The tiny nun brought world attention to the plight of the poor through her quiet determination.

The roots of President Teddy Roosevelt's determination started with a childhood ailment. Severe asthma limited his ability to play like other kids, and as he lay in bed struggling to breathe, Roosevelt was afraid to go to sleep for fear he wouldn't wake up. Yet Roosevelt was determined to become strong mentally and physically. His desire to become self-sufficient fortified him through a daily exercise routine and hours of weight lifting. He became an avid reader and absorbed books on every conceivable subject. As a Harvard student, Roosevelt became known for his energy and enthusiasm.

Thousands of businesses that statistically should have failed are successful today because of the determination of their owners:

- In his first three years in the auto business, Henry Ford went bankrupt twice.
- Coca-Cola sold only 400 Cokes in its first year.
- Apple Computer was rejected by Hewlett-Packard and Atari.
- Inventor Chester Carlson pounded the streets for years before he could find backers for his Xerox photocopying process.

Today we live in a culture of instant gratification, where the attributes of patience and determination are hard to find. We need to be more like the young college graduate who was determined to find a position with a reputable company. In the interview process she faced continual rejection, yet her determination helped keep her goals in mind. One busy personnel manager, flooded with applications, suggested the hopeful applicant check back in 10 years. "No problem," the young woman responded. "Would a morning or afternoon interview work best for you?"

MACKAY'S MORAL:

Be like a postage stamp. Stick to it until you get there.

Chapter 5

WINNING

win (win), **won, winning** . . . *v.i.* **1.** to gain the victory **2.** to finish first in a race or contest **3.** to succeed by effort.

Neil Steinberg, a newspaper reporter, published a provocative and amusing book, *Complete & Utter Failure: A Celebration of Also-Rans, Runners-Up, Never-Weres & Total Flops.* By far the largest section is about the national spelling bee, "an institutionalized failure," "a distillation of the ills of the American education system."

With 60 pages devoted to trashing it, Steinberg has a lot to say about what's wrong with the spelling bee. For one thing, despite endless assurances by every adult in sight that all the nine million participants are "winners," Steinberg counts 8,999,999 losers, some of whom burst into tears when they get a word wrong, or relieve their frustrations by duking out a punching bag thoughtfully provided in the Comfort Room immediately offstage.

"I struggle to find some sort of meaning, some utility in this vast expenditure of effort," Steinberg laments. After all, who has to know how to wing words like "thanatophidia" or "abiogenist"? You look 'em up. Better to spend the time practicing the violin. You can't look that up.

The point of the contest is not to find the best speller, but to have a contest, to enlist kids in the adult world of rote learning, cutthroat competition, humiliating defeat, and/or (at 8,999,999 to one odds) meaningless victory. "All the trouble and effort to name a spelling bee champion in order to have a spelling bee champion named. It is an end in itself."

Well, let's see if the same criticism holds up when we look at another kids' contest.

Not so long ago I watched the opening events of the Special Olympics.

Physically and mentally challenged young people from all over the world get together and participate in athletic events.

The point of the event is not to find the best athlete. None of the participants will set any world records. Their athletic achievements might be looked at as essentially meaningless, but they capture the spirit of athletics, which is as much about participating as it is about competing.

Should they have taken Steinberg's advice and put in their time on a more practical pursuit, like the violin? Should they seek to develop skills where they stand better odds of finishing first?

No.

The first definition of winning is not "to finish first," it is "to gain the victory."

That might mean finishing first, but it might just as well mean:

- taking part,
- having fun,
- setting a goal,
- making the attempt,
- having the support, love, and admiration of your friends and family,
- being the best you can be,
- being welcomed as an equal and learning that everyone counts,
- making a personal sacrifice,
- experiencing pain, setbacks, defeats, and having the courage to risk humiliation,
- testing your own limits,
- performing in front of an audience,
- making new friends,
- breaking through to a new level of performance,
- traveling to new places,

- encouraging others,
- sharing the experience, and
- hearing the applause.

Those are equally important elements of winning. Maybe they're easier for us to see when they involve the kids who are physically challenged rather than kids who have the skills to spell improbable words.

That's because it's so obvious that the Special Olympics kids are having the time of their lives. The principal physical danger at these games is the omnipresent possibility of being hugged to death. As for the spelling contest, Steinberg points out that, "The bee retains the appeal it had as the symbol of the American Dream. A full quarter of the contestants come from ethnic immigrant families . . . Chinese, Koreans, Thais, Cambodians, Hispanics, and subcontinental Indians. They are the same crowd that excel at schools across the country, their families having instilled in them the fierce drive to succeed and the love of education so often faded in those who have been here long enough to take education for granted."

Complete and utter failure? Steinberg knows better. And so do the Special Olympics kids. They seem to have a pretty solid grasp of why they're there and what winning is really all about.

MACKAY'S MORAL:

There's much more to winning than finishing first.

Chapter 6

TRUST YOURSELF

Irwin Jacobs graduated from a public high school in a section of town that was on the borderline between working class and the class that couldn't get enough work. Jacobs didn't like school. He had other plans. After much pleading from his father, Jacobs agreed to attend the University of Minnesota. The deal was this:

"Irwin, just give it a try. If you decide you don't like it, well, then you don't have to stay."

Irwin gave it a shot. Perhaps it was not his best shot. He quit after one day. One day. That was it. His next move was to buy some sports equipment—fancy fishing poles or skis, I think—at a liquidation sale. He resold them a day later for 10 times what he paid for them. To Irwin Jacobs, that was a lot better way to spend a day than his day at the U. School has been out for him ever since.

As far as I know, Jacobs doesn't own a fishing pole, but he does own a couple of companies that manufacture fishing boats, and other boats. And other companies. Net worth: estimated in excess of $250 million.

Then there's Bill Gates. If you've heard about him, you may want to take up a collection for Jacobs. Gates dropped out of Harvard at age 20 and opened up a business in his garage. He called it Microsoft. He is now the single richest person in the United States, if not in the world, with a personal fortune measured in the tens of billions.

Now, I'm a sucker for stories like that, and I'm not alone. It is a phenomenon of American life that we are suspicious of intellect. We all like to hear about people who had mediocre records in school and then blossomed into big-time success. We like them almost as much as the horror stories about the high school heroes who hit the skids. Why?

Because there are a lot more of us who were mediocre types than were brains. Also, high school is a time of maximum insecurity. Not being among the smartest, it was easy to feel less than admiration for the kids who were. And who probably had not yet developed the smooth veneer that turneth away envy.

The popularity of the "smart is dumb" theory is understandable, but don't confuse the Irwin Jacobs–Bill Gates type of success stories with the belief that it pays to be ignorant. These guys are smart all right, they're just a different kind of smart.

They trusted themselves. They learned what mattered to them and totally ignored those things that didn't. Few of us have that kind of self-confidence. School held no charms for a poor kid who could double his money overnight trading fishing poles. That doesn't make him dumb. Just a lot more sure of his own talents than the rest of us.

Take a look at your own high school class. What has become of the good athletes and scholars, the class president, the science whiz? My guess is that they have been able to transfer their success in school to success in their careers. It's not that the subjects we study in school have direct application to our jobs. Few of us have occasion to use our high school German or dissect a frog in our daily lives.

School is about learning, all right. But it's learning to work a system, learning self-discipline, learning to deal with other people, learning to pay attention, learning what you like to do, what you don't like to do, what you do well, what you do badly.

Sometimes, tough family situations or inadequate school facilities have been a major factor in holding us back. Sometimes, for the Irwin Jacobs and Bill Gates of the world, school just doesn't offer the kind of real-world training that turns them on.

Jacobs and Gates have a special talent. They believe in themselves. They believe in themselves so strongly that for them school was a barrier, keeping them from their dreams, rather than a means of preparing for the work-a-day world. They were right about that. For them, school was work. Work was never really work at all.

However, things haven't always worked out so well for some indifferent scholars.

George Armstrong Custer, who led the Seventh Cavalry at the Battle of Little Big Horn, graduated at the bottom of his class at West Point.

MACKAY'S MORAL:

The only things that are truly work are the things we don't do well.

Chapter 7

TAKE A LESSON FROM MY FOLKS: NEVER STOP LEARNING

If at first you're afraid to fail, then you won't ever succeed.

One of the greatest things my parents did for me was to encourage every one of my ambitions, even if they appeared to be overreaching. They listened to my dreams of being a golf champ or a basketball pro, cheered them on, and then—what really counted—put their money where their mouths were. They made those dreams seem a lot more attainable by giving me lessons in golf and basketball.

I don't think my folks gave me those lessons because they shared my fantasies of becoming the next Ben Hogan or George Mikan. They did it so I could find out how to be the best Harvey Mackay possible.

From the age of seven or eight, I had lessons, in addition to golf and basketball, in boxing, dancing, swimming, skating, skiing, tennis, baseball, Ping-Pong, and bowling. I also got help from experts in public speaking, piano playing, and writing. And I have no doubt that if I had expressed interest in card tricks, scuba diving, or astronomy, they would have found teachers for those, too.

Yes, I was privileged, but I see plenty of dads and moms making sure that their kids get to Scouts and Little League and community programs, motivated by the same good reasons as my folks: to give their children knowledge and to create a habit of learning.

There is more to learn today than ever. As the amount of information in the world doubles approximately every five years, it takes more and more effort just to run in place. Moreover, companies are cutting back, trying to do as much or more with fewer people. The more talents you have, the more valuable you are. Finally, if you want to attract and retain increasingly knowledgeable, intelligent, demanding, and sophisticated customers/consumers, you have to be as smart as they are.

That's why my parents' support has proved so valuable. Some of the lessons they encouraged sharpened the skills I was born with. Some developed abilities I might never have had. But they also taught me to enjoy learning for its own sake.

I learned what a pleasure it is to be taken seriously. Any coach worth his salt has an emotional and psychological investment in his players that's often as rewarding as the play itself. There is nothing as ego building, as challenging and inspiring to a kid as having a grown-up treat him or her as if what he or she does really matters.

I learned that whatever you do is a lot more enjoyable when you do it well. It's fun to go to a golf driving range and hit a bucket of balls. It's a lot more fun to hit them so they travel exactly where you want them to go. What I learned in those long-ago sessions is very much with me today. Forty years ago, I took at least 100 golf lessons from the dean of Minnesota golf professionals, Les Bolstad. I still refer to my notes of yesteryear, and they continue to increase my knowledge and pleasure in the game.

I learned how much pleasure it is possible to derive from work. Many young people seem to think that once you leave school and enter the world of work, your horizon becomes narrow and grim. But working with professionals in any field, and observing how much they enjoy what they're doing, gives you an incredibly positive notion of how life can be lived.

Most important, *I learned not to be afraid to try something new*. Obviously, I wasn't equally competent at everything I tried. But I certainly realized my capacity to be a beginner at anything. A friend of mine once told me that she was too afraid to take an art history course in college because of the lab requirement. Artistic ability wasn't required—you just had to cut and paste, the idea being that you would learn something about Monet's and Mondrian's composition by moving shapes around by yourself—but my friend couldn't muster the courage to take that course. She was afraid to fail. This is the greatest handicap of all.

MACKAY'S MORAL:

Be like the turtle . . . if it didn't stick its neck out,
it wouldn't get anywhere at all.

Chapter 8

ALL THINGS COME TO THOSE WHO GO AFTER THEM

Will Rogers once said, "Even if you're on the right track, you'll get run over if you just sit there."

Knowledge is only useful when put into action. You can't just sit there and wait for your ship to come in . . . you've got to swim out to it before the pier rots.

We can learn a lot about action by looking at insects. Consider the bee. It will make visits to 125 clover heads to make one gram of honey. That comes to about 25,000 trips for bees to make only one pound of honey. Ants are admirable creatures as well. They're not concerned about their stature but go about their diligent, tireless work of storing up food for their colony.

Lillian Vernon, who's been a friend of mine over the years, was a 24-year-old newlywed seeking some extra income for her family when she spent $2,000 of her wedding money on an advertisement in *Seventeen* magazine, promoting monogrammed handbags and belts. The orders came, business grew, and today her mail-order catalog company, Lillian Vernon Corporation, has annual sales of $240 million and ships 50,000 orders daily during its peak holiday season.

Ted and Dorothy Hustead likewise had a dream in 1931: to open a drug store in a town with a good school, a Catholic church, and a doctor. They chose Wall, South Dakota, a middle-of-nowhere town situated between the Badlands and the

Black Hills. After a long dusty year in which few visitors stopped at their drug store, they were forced to do some serious soul searching. They came up with an idea to lure parched visitors to their establishment and acted on it, posting FREE ICE WATER AT WALL DRUG signs all over the area. The signs soon became a novelty and were placed further and further away. Today, Wall Drug signs can be seen all over the world from Korea to the North Pole. During peak season, four to six thousand people visit daily.

You don't have to be famous or the CEO of a large corporation to have an idea and act on it.

One of the best lines on the silver screen about the importance of action came from Yoda, the Jedi Knight trainer in the *Star Wars* sequel, *The Empire Strikes Back*. While teaching Luke Skywalker about the power of the Force, Yoda says, "Luke, there is no try; there is either do or not do."

Here's a scenario you might recognize at your workplace:

There once were four people named Everybody, Somebody, Anybody, and Nobody. An important job had to be done, and Everybody was sure that Somebody would do it. Anybody could have done it, but Nobody did it. Somebody got angry about that, because it was Everybody's job. Everybody thought Anybody could do it and that Somebody would do it. But Nobody realized that Everybody thought Somebody would do it. It ended up that Everybody blamed Somebody when Nobody did what Anybody could have done.

Be somebody who makes things happen. How? In the words of Nike, "Just do it."

MACKAY'S MORAL:

Ideas without action are like being all dressed
up with no place to go.

EARNING THE
STAMP OF APPROVAL

Chapter 9

FATHER OF THE GROOM

My son, David, is a film director. Like any normal father, I've been trying to sell him my movie idea, but he just won't listen.

"You're an envelope guy, Dad," he says. "I'm a movie guy. Do I try to horn in on your #10s? Do I try to tell you what kind of glue tastes best on your flaps?"

"Well, no," I say, "but I've got this terrific idea."

"Dad, do me a favor, will you? Take it over to MGM."

How like a serpent's tooth, etc. What he doesn't know is that I already tried MGM, and they don't like it either.

Maybe you will.

This is the age of political correctitude, sensitivity, equal treatment, right? Okay, we've had *Father of the Bride* and we've had *Father of the Bride Part II*. So what about *Father of the Groom?*

When my son, David, went down the aisle a few years ago, and I saw some of his friends for the first time in 10 years, I got this inspiration. . . .

SCENE 1

Distant shot of the ocean waves gently lapping the shore on a perfect California day.

Camera moves up and over the shoreline to reveal the grounds of an elegant oceanfront hotel where guests are mingling at a formal wedding party.

Camera pans group of male friends of groom in wedding party laughing and joking with each other.

Camera pauses on Billy Yates.

Was it just a bad hair day, or did Billy have a thing about purple hair?

Billy rolls up tuxedo sleeves revealing tattoos to admiring audience.

Shot of mother and father of the groom (Mackay) reacting to Billy, while pretending not to be reacting to Billy.

Shot of Billy snickering at mother and father's nonreaction reaction.

Fade out.

SCENE 2 *(Flashback, eight years earlier)*

Establishing shot of medium-sized manufacturing company. Sign on roof reads MACKAY ENVELOPE CORPORATION.

Cut to interior shot of door to private office. Sign on door reads HARVEY MACKAY.

Cut to office. Jumbles of papers are scattered hither and yon. There are large stacks of books—or rather, a book—everywhere.

Close-up of book reveals title: *Swim with the Sharks Without Being Eaten Alive*, #1 bestseller by Harvey Mackay.

Mackay is seated behind desk across from nervous young man. It's Billy! Billy is dressed as one would expect a young man to dress when calling upon an old fud who is supposed to be an expert in providing career advice. Mackay plays the role to the rafters, spouting aphorisms.

"Dig your well before you stub your toe," says Mackay. "Wait a minute, that's not it. . . ."

When Billy is able to get a word in edgewise, he reveals he spent five years at a state university, winding up a few credits short of a college degree. Of modest means, in high school he ran a bike-repair shop from his garage. Most recently, he's worked as a busboy. As he speaks he becomes less nervous. With his enthusiasm, energy, and imagination, he's an extremely likable young man.

"No one ever got thirsty going backwards," says Mackay. "That isn't right, either . . . er. . . . What do you really like to do, Billy?"

"Windsurf, music, sell things, surf the Web."

"Surf the what?"

"Surf the Web. I think it's got real potential," says Billy.

Tight shot on Mackay. Mackay could have been Benjamin in *The Graduate* hearing about "Plastics, plastics." He looks totally befuddled.

Cut to:

SCENE 3 *(The present)*

Close-up on cover of *Fortune* magazine. Pages open to picture inside of Billy, hair normal, but still not exactly stepping out of *GQ*. He's wearing faded jeans, black boots, and what is probably a $40 T-shirt. Cutline on the full-page photo reads "Billy Yates, 32, president, Zoom Software, Inc., Eugene, Oregon. Zoom's projected 1999 revenues: $60 million. Zoom's stock went up 600 percent in 1998 and continues to rise and split like bakers' yeast. Today, Billy could buy twenty restaurants like the one he once bused in."

Cut to:

SCENE 4 *(The not-too-distant future)*

Wide establishing shot of large manufacturing firm. Sign on the roof reads ZOOM SOFTWARE, INC.

Cut to interior shot of door to private office. Sign on the door reads BILLY.

Cut to office. It is neat, very high tech, computer screens flashing everywhere. Billy is seated behind desk in casual clothes. An elderly gentleman in a business suit is seated across from him. It's Mackay!

"So, Harvey," says Billy. "What can I do for you?"

Mackay appears to be concentrating very hard.

"You'll never stub your toe walking backwards," says Mackay.

"That's right!" says Billy. "Wonderful advice!"

"Dig your well before you're thirsty!" says Mackay, triumphantly.

"Marvelous!" says Billy. "What wise counsel. Now, I have some advice for you."

"What?" says Mackay.

"Envelopes, envelopes," says Billy. "You can only use an envelope once and then you have to throw it away."

Mackay's brow furrows, but gradually the light dawns and a wide smile breaks across his face.

Freeze frame.

The End.

Roll the credits.

MACKAY'S MORAL:

Clothes don't make the man. The man makes the man. Welcome to the new millennium. (David, I'm telling you, this movie is gonna be bigger than *Titanic*.)

Chapter 10

IF IT'S A TIE,
YOU LOSE

My kids may not vote the way I'd like them to, think my jokes are funny, or like my kind of music, but at least they've learned not to give me neckties for gifts.

You can learn, too.

For years, whenever corporate giving comes up in a sales meeting, I've been begging, pleading, screaming . . .

Don't be boring!

Don't be predictable.

Be a differentiator.

When Ted Koppel came to the University of Minnesota to address the annual alumni association meeting, it was a thrill for me to introduce him. I did my homework and found out he was a tennis junkie, and we played some tennis before his talk. After it was over, I wanted to thank him. I knew if I wrote him the standard note, it wouldn't make it out of the mail room, so I overnighted him a five-foot, fifteen-pound tennis racket, and a tennis ball about the size of a watermelon with this note:

> Here's to the star of *Nightline*.
> To help him improve his sightline.
> Just line up the ball and whack it.
> You'll never miss one with this racket.

To which I received this reply 48 hours later:

Dear Harvey,
When a man has real class, then he'll show it.
Everyone in his sphere tends to know it.
Tell me, why would he choose
To risk all and lose
By pretending that he is a poet.

He signed it "6–0, 6–0, 6–0. Racket and ball are great. Thanks for everything."

Incidentally, Koppel gave me a very complimentary endorsement for my first book, *Swim with the Sharks Without Being Eaten Alive*, possibly because of the playful exchange with the racket and ball. All I know is his jacket endorsement was the first biggie I received, and without question sent me on my way to an unbelievably successful book. I am eternally grateful.

The best time to be creative is when it's least expected. Thanksgiving cards still pack a bigger punch than Christmas cards because they stand out from the crowd. One of our salespeople learned that a customer's new baby boy had been born that day. Within hours he had delivered a toy to their home . . . for his two-year-old sister, knowing she might be in need of some attention.

When someone is in the hospital, they're especially needy. We send a bright red balloon so big it will barely fit through the door of the room. Filled with helium and a basket full of goodies, these monsters are the talk of the hospital.

A great time to be imaginative is when you've opened a new account and want to show your appreciation. Forget the standard letter from the CEO. Why not try what we sometimes do at Mackay Envelope? Within 24 hours of receiving a first-time order, we will arrange delivery of a 30 to 40-foot telegram saying "Thank You" in 15 different languages. Believe me, that one makes it to the bulletin board, not the trash bin like a boilerplate letter would.

Corporate gift giving is wrapped up in the concept of staying close to your customer. To do the job right, you have to know that customer as a living, breathing human being, with likes and dislikes, interests, a family, and a background, so you can knock their socks off when a remembrance package shows up.

The funny thing about gifts is that 99 percent of us think they have to be expensive to be appreciated. A gift that shows you have taken the trouble to pay attention and have a genuine personal interest in your customer says a lot more than a dollar sign.

How about a simple card thanking them for their friendship and patronage, accompanied by a small sample of your products? For instance, a publisher could send out coffee-table books, a winery might send a bottle of wine, and I know a taxi-cab company that sends out coupon books.

You're an accountant? Send a brand-name pen "good for marking off tax deductions." A stockbroker? Send a portfolio.

You don't have to emulate *Lethal Weapon* film director Richard Donner, who a couple of years ago gave producer Joel Silver a customized pinball machine. It cost $50,000 and was programmed to bark obscenities and messages from Demi Moore and Arnold Schwarzenegger.

For instance, take two somewhat tired concepts: (*a*) candy, and (*b*) your logo—and combine them. A couple of years ago Bell South Mobility sent out cellular phones made out of chocolate and stamped with the company logo. They didn't work very well but they sure did taste good.

Here's another way to turn a business cliché into an imaginative gift. Given today's business practices, chances are people on your gift list grew up in another state. Every state has its food specialties. Send them something from back home. Barry Shlachter of Fort Worth sends out "Texan in Exile Survival Rations" to his old buddies from Texas who no longer live there.

Years ago I had a customer whose entire life was built around golf. He not only played around the clock, the only clothes he seemed to own were golf clothes and the only jokes he knew were golf jokes. His idol was Arnold Palmer. I'm a golfer, but I know Arnold Palmer about as well as I know Arnold Schwarzenegger. Still, when Palmer wrote a book, I busted my putter getting a friend to contact a friend to contact a friend who did know him and got him to personally inscribe a few lines from "Arnold Palmer to my good friend, Joe Duffer." For 15 years, Joe has been dining out on his close personal relationship to his "good friend" Arnold Palmer, and for 15 years the envelope orders have just kept rolling in.

This isn't rocket science we're talking here. It's common sense stuff. We can all create our own Rolodex.

Write it down. Birthdays, anniversaries, kids' names, their graduation dates, interests, memberships, the whole bit.

That's step one.

Step two is to use it. Imaginatively.

Step three is to get out your order book.

MACKAY'S MORAL:

If you're creative, you'll show it.

If you've got class, you'll let them know it.

There's nothing that results in indignation,

More than a deadly lack of imagination.

Chapter 11

HELP WANTED

Anyone who has ever served in the armed forces can recall a variation on this familiar theme: "All right. I want volunteers to clean the head, swab the deck, peel the spuds. That means you, you, and you."

I can understand why this kind of experience may have made many of us gun-shy whenever we hear the word "volunteer." However, if I can adopt my crass mercantile persona for a moment, let me suggest that nothing will benefit you more personally—to say nothing of the people you will benefit—than if you become an active community volunteer.

When I was about 20 years old, my father made a point of telling me that he thought one-fourth of my life should be devoted to volunteerism. I have followed that advice, volunteering with a variety of organizations over the years, from serving on the boards of the Minnesota Orchestra and Guthrie Theater to raising money to send the University of Minnesota Concert Band to China.

Every nonprofit organization needs people and money. They need the people to get the money.

Fund-raising is crucial. If you are willing to become a fund-raiser, you will enhance your own skills in two significant ways:

1. Selling.

If you want to learn how to sell, here's how to start at the primal level: Ask people for money. I can't think of a better sales training program than several dozen rejections. Oh, you say you're a lawyer/doctor/accountant and you don't have to sell? Dream on. Maybe that was true 20 years ago, but not anymore.

In my town, former federal court judges are not above running ads on television. You'll also see doctors' pictures on billboards and buses, and accountants peddling their wares in the local papers. And if it's true here, it's true everywhere.

2. Networking.

No matter what you do for a living, you need customers. The best way to get them is to get to know them. That means meeting as many people as possible. The nice thing about fundraising is that the people you meet tend to have funds, and people with funds make the best customers.

When I was chairman of the American Cancer Society for the state of Minnesota, I volunteered to travel the state for one year and put on eight cancer informational clinics. Of course, there were professional medical people with me all the time. I can't say these docs have become great generators of envelope business, but after many years I can still pick up a phone and call any one of them and get a "best in the country" medical referral whenever I need one. That kind of network is worth more than all the #10s in the warehouse.

We're entering a new era in this country when it comes to volunteerism. Government's role as the provider of social services is declining. The need for volunteers is increasing.

You don't have to have an ulterior motive or be a peddler as I've suggested here to be a valuable volunteer. Nonprofit organizations are delighted to accept volunteers who are just plain nice people and want to help others in all kinds of ways.

Helping people gives you a high similar to the endorphins you experience when running and competing in sports.

People who do volunteer work and help other people on a regular basis have a healthier outlook on life. They are more inclined to be go-getters and consistently report being happier. I have seen results of a study on this, and all the people interviewed emphasized how volunteering made them feel better. I agree.

One of my favorite volunteer organizations is S.C.O.R.E.,

the Service Corps of Retired Executives, 800-634-0245. I try to mention them in every book I write. There are chapters all over the country, which are mapped out on its Web site at www.score.org. This group is made up of retired executives who were successful in business and now act as consultants to people with an entrepreneurial bent who need some guidance putting together a business plan or marketing their ideas.

Young, old, professional, student, teacher, it doesn't matter. Volunteer. And if you missed out on painting the hatches or raking the leaves when you were in the service, I guarantee you'll find those jobs are still open, too.

MACKAY'S MORAL:

The best way to help yourself is to help others.

Chapter 12

THE FIXER

If you're a minister, your signature event is your Sunday sermon. That's the part of the job that's most visible to the largest number of parishioners. It's also the most fun.

However, there is a lot more to successful ministering than performing in front of an audience. There are very successful ministers who aren't Billy Sunday in the pulpit. They are popular with their congregations because they never neglect the countless small chores, like committee meetings, Bible studies, and hospital visitations.

There's no part of the job that can build security and loyalty like visitation. And there is never a lack of opportunity to do it. Every congregation has elderly and infirm members.

It would be very hard for parishioners to vote against the person who stood at the bedside with them when Dad passed away or who held their hand and prayed with them just before a major operation. Unsurprisingly, members tend to value those moments more than a fiery sermon.

Richard Clearwaters was pastor at the Fourth Baptist Church in Minneapolis. Dr. Clearwaters did not trim his theological views to win approval. He left the conservative Baptists (the conservative Baptists!) because they were too liberal.

Despite his uncompromising attitude on matters theological, his ministry was huge. He ran a large church, a private school (kindergarten through eighth grade), a seminary, and a radio station.

He had a full plate. Still, he found the time to make visitation calls. Every day.

The admitting clerks at the hospitals all knew him and would let him look at the list of new patients. If the name sounded vaguely familiar, Clearwaters would stop by their room.

One of my friends told me, "We've never set foot in his church, Harvey, yet he's called on my wife every time she's been hospitalized. Our own pastor has rarely come to see her."

It's no wonder Doc Clearwaters lasted about 50 years with Fourth Baptist.

Politicians love the limelight even more than pastors.

The speeches, the awards, the interviews, the media coverage. It's all pretty heady stuff. But every now and then, you see a pol who makes you wonder how he ever gets elected in this TV age. He never makes a speech, never sponsors important legislation, no charisma, bad hair, and still, he's been around forever.

I'd be willing to bet this is a guy who does a great job on constituent service, the kind who pays a constituent's parking ticket out of his own pocket just to let the disgruntled voter think he had it "taken care of."

I know a successful real estate agent who has a similar habit that set her apart from her competitors. Every day she makes it a point to make contact with a former client. It could be a phone call, a letter, or a personal meeting. She will not call it quits for the day until she has made that contact.

"It's simple arithmetic," she says. "The average American changes homes once every five years. There are a lot of people I've sold three houses to."

Most of the real estate business is referrals. Because she stays in touch with her old clients, she gets more than her share of referrals from people she has done business with previously. Now she's getting calls from sons and daughters of clients buying their first homes!

Every company has someone they call the Fixer. The Fixer can get it for you wholesale, can get your brother-in-law bailed out of jail in the middle of the night or come up with tickets to the concert that has been sold out for months.

Top management doesn't know how he or she does it. They

don't want to know. But they're delighted to accept the fruits of their labor. The Fixer is never at the top of the organization chart, there is no job description for what they do, and the title is a joke—but it could be the most secure job in the company.

MACKAY'S MORAL:

The reason they call them troubleshooters is they have a yen for gunning down problems.

THE CUTTING EDGE

Chapter 13

PUTTING THE DIFFERENT IN DIFFERENTIATOR

Charles Walgreen, who founded the drugstore chain, worked as a pharmacist on the south side of Chicago in 1901. When a customer phoned in to have a prescription refilled, Walgreen would take down the information and then continue his conversation with the caller. After a while, the customer would say, "Excuse me for a minute, there's someone at the door." Who would that someone be? A delivery boy with a package from Walgreen's. It was the customer's prescription.

Walgreen had a few other innovative notions about doing business. He invented the soda fountain and the lunch counter. From that one store Walgreen's has grown to 94,000 employees and over $13.4 billion in sales annually.

I never stop talking about a friend of mine, Don Bosold, a salesman who lives in Florida. He told me that every day, before he starts his rounds, he reaches into his wallet and pulls out a card on which he has written a single word: "Astonish." Obviously, that's what Mr. Walgreen had in mind, too.

American business success stories have not always consisted solely of downsizings and restructurings. There are countless cases where smart people continue to sell and resell the most mundane products and services year in and year out.

They win their customers by cleverly differentiating themselves from their competition.

Take United Parcel Service. Every day every driver of a UPS truck washes his or her truck. Does it help get the packages there any faster? Of course not. But it does send a message. Even when you're doing something as unexciting as delivering packages, you can still take pride in your work, in your appearance, in doing things right. If you take the trouble to wash your truck every day, doesn't it stand to reason you will take the trouble to handle your customers' packages properly?

An article in *Fortune* asked "Is Herb Kelleher America's Best CEO?" The answer is: maybe, maybe not, but Kelleher certainly belongs on everyone's short list. Kelleher is the head of Southwest Airlines, which, like UPS, is a commodity delivery service, only in this case the commodity is people. Airlines don't compete on the basis of service, they compete on the basis of nonservice. Each tries to find ways to stuff more people into their "tubes," while searching for new ways to cut down on what passes for amenities. One airline is pretty much like another, but Southwest has managed to stand out from the pack, and not because they're serving haute cuisine. Southwest fare is spartan even by airline standards. Peanuts and crackers. They don't even provide assigned seating.

What's different is the corporate culture. It would astonish even my friend who starts each day with "Astonish." Ticket agents will hump baggage. Pilots will take tickets. Flight attendants have been known to pop out of overhead storage bins. Passengers have been awarded prizes for having the biggest holes in their socks. The peanuts and crackers are likely to be served with Shamu the Whale napkins and party favors. Kelleher himself has been known to drop in on a flight, pumping hands and passing out those fabled peanuts. He has not yet made the sort of fashion statement he is noted for in his meetings with employees, where he has appeared dressed as Elvis or the Easter Bunny.

So much for the jokes. The bottom line is no joke.

Southwest has won the "Department of Transportation Triple Crown" in the past: most on-time flights, best baggage handling, highest customer satisfaction. And unlike competitors, Southwest's bonds are investment grade, not jokes.

What accounts for it all? In the words of a Harvard case study, Southwest is "differentiating itself through its focus on service, operations, cost control, marketing, its people and its corporate culture."

There's that word again: "differentiating."

A lot of companies developed quirky little habits in their early years and then abandoned the effort. IBMers are no longer required to wear white shirts. Hershey has finally started advertising. Hathaway's eye-patch man is all but a memory. Parker pens have lost their distinctive hooded design. Times change. But I wonder, if in losing those distinctive traits, those companies didn't lose something more valuable: the characteristics that differentiate them from all the others.

MACKAY'S MORAL:

Take some of Charles Walgreen's medicine
and be a differentiator.

Chapter 14

CREATIVITY KILLERS

Want to know how to kill creativity? Go to a cocktail party. No, I'm not talking about tossing back Bahama Mamas until the only joke you can think of to tell is the latest Doonesbury cartoon. I'm talking about *listening*. Cocktail parties are all about unwinding, and when people unwind they tell you things. The thing they tell you most is what happened at the office that put them down—then stopped them cold on the path toward creativity and left them feeling disempowered, demotivated, and defunct.

It's amazing, if you go to as many schmooze-fests as I have over the years, how succinctly people will explain to you how their boss failed them at the crucial moment when they needed encouragement to go forward. Here are some of the creativity killers I've heard at receptions, conferences, seminars, speeches, and cocktail parties that are guaranteed to make the person on the other end of the conversation go dead:

1. It's not in the budget.
2. The boss will never go for it.
3. Great idea! Let's form a committee to tackle it.
4. It will never work.
5. That's against our policy.
6. Who will we get to do it?
7. Let's think about it for a while.
8. Let's discuss it some other time.
9. Why not leave well enough alone?
10. It's too late to fix it now.
11. It's too soon to fix it now.

12. We have done it this way for so many years, and we still make a profit.
13. Why fix it if it isn't broken?
14. We tried it five years ago and it didn't work.
15. That's not how we do things around here.
16. That's the kind of idea that cost your predecessor her job.
17. It will take a long time to research this idea.
18. That's not my job.
19. The competition already does it that way.
20. The competition doesn't do it that way.
21. Let's let the competition try it first and see what happens.
22. That isn't in our job descriptions.
23. If we do it, they'll wonder why we didn't do it sooner.
24. It will create more work for the rest of us.
25. Sounds like a good idea. . . . Let's run it by legal.

> ### MACKAY'S MORAL:
>
> Cowards die a thousand deaths. Unfortunately, cowards kill thousands of creative ideas before death catches up with them.

Chapter 15

FUZZY LOGIC

Welcome to the twentieth century where the iron formulas of science continue to play catch-up with the concept of change. Einstein really started it all. He threw Newtonian physics overboard and proved that if you go far enough out into space, space bends and the rules of time, mass, motion, and energy change.

"Fuzzy logic" is the application of this concept to mechanical engineering. The principle behind fuzzy logic is this: The most effective decision making is not always made according to predetermined rules. There are too many variables. The best rules aren't rules. They aren't set in concrete. They bend. The best decisions are made at the last possible instant when the greatest number of variables can be predicted with the greatest degree of accuracy.

You'll find fuzzy logic in the minicomputers that regulate appliances like vacuum cleaners and washing machines. Through sensors, fuzzy logic can adjust the temperature of the water and the speed of the agitator in your washer according to the amount of dirt in the stuff you dumped in it.

Each of us has a built-in fuzzy logic sensor. Some are more sensitive than others. Take baseball. The best hitters are those who are able to absorb all the variables—the type of pitch, its speed, the location of the ball—and make the tiny, final, split-second adjustments in their swing that will enable them to sock it on the nose.

The rest of us .190 hitters would sometimes do a lot better if we were to make our own logic a little fuzzier.

If you are a manager, do you use fuzzy logic, or are you a

paint-by-the-numbers type who never lets his crayon stray over the outline? For instance, when the workload in your department increases or when you sense morale in your people is sagging, is it business as usual or do you act to crank up their batteries? If you don't, if you never change your attitude, day in and day out, good times, bad times, if you're the Great Stone Face, you aren't adapting to changing conditions. You aren't using fuzzy logic. The result is that you may not be getting the most out of your people.

When the new order cometh and you have to ask your people to do things differently, do you help them adjust? Good managers know when to step in and use the hands-on approach and when to lay off.

If you're in a position of authority, do you use fuzzy logic? Are you able to delegate decision-making power downwards to the people actually on the firing line, or do you jealously guard power up the ladder until it reaches you?

Are you giving your salespeople authority to deal, to make reasonable price and delivery concessions to meet customer needs?

Are you giving your designers and engineers authority to select components and systems?

Are you giving your marketing people authority to plan and execute programs and promotions?

What about other workers who deal directly with customers?

At TGI Friday's, waiters and waitresses are encouraged to bend the rules and do whatever it takes to keep customers happy, even if that means running to the supermarket to get a can of sardines to make a sardine sandwich. Other restaurants give their waiters and waitresses discretion to placate unhappy customers with free desserts.

Fuzzy logic is just a cute, maybe too cute, way of describing the means for making more effective decisions by defining rule making to include the right to bend the rules to meet changing conditions. Fuzzy logic means hanging loose, staying flexible.

Consistency used to be the hobgoblin of little minds. Now we give it another name: micromanaging. A solution for every problem and every solution written down in the rulebook. Rigid consistency has been programmed even out of little machines. Program it out of your system, too. Ruffle your rulebook. Get with it. Get fuzzy.

MACKAY'S MORAL:

There are only two rules. Rule One: The rules keep changing. Rule Two: The only rule that doesn't change is rule one.

Chapter 16

SUCCESS IS GETTING UP MORE THAN YOU FALL DOWN

I'm constantly asked what I think is the secret of success. Well, it's a lot of things but at the top of my list are two beliefs: *(a)* you need to be a hungry fighter, and *(b)* a hungry fighter never quits. I've learned over the years that success is largely hanging on after others have let go.

When you study the truly successful people, you'll see that they have made plenty of mistakes, but when they were knocked down, they kept getting up . . . and up . . . and up. Like the Energizer Bunny keeps going . . . and going . . . and going.

Abraham Lincoln failed in business, lost numerous elections and his sweetheart, and had a nervous breakdown. But he never quit. He kept on trying and became, according to many, our greatest president.

- Dr. Seuss's first children's book was rejected by 23 publishers.
- Michael Jordan was cut from his high school basketball team.
- Henry Ford failed and went broke five times before he finally succeeded.

- Franklin D. Roosevelt was struck down by polio but he never quit.
- Helen Keller, totally deaf and blind, graduated cum laude from Radcliffe College, and went on to become a famous author and lecturer.
- Adam Clark labored 40 years writing his commentary on the Holy Scriptures.
- The *History of the Decline and Fall of the Roman Empire* took Edward Gibbon 26 painstaking years to complete.
- Ernest Hemingway is said to have revised *The Old Man and the Sea* manuscript 80 times before submitting it for publication.
- It took Noah Webster 36 years to compile *Webster's Dictionary*.
- The University of Bern rejected Albert Einstein's Ph.D. dissertation, saying it was irrelevant and fanciful.
- Johnny Unitas was cut by the Pittsburgh Steelers, but he kept his dream alive by working construction and playing amateur football while staying in contact with every NFL team. The Baltimore Colts finally responded and he became one of the greatest quarterbacks to ever play the game.
- Richard Hooker worked seven years on the humorous war novel, *M*A*S*H*, only to have it rejected by 21 publishers.
- Charles Goodyear spent every last dollar over five years filled with experiments to try and develop a rubber life preserver before he succeeded.

I love the story about the high school basketball coach who was attempting to motivate his players to persevere through a difficult season. Halfway through the season he stood before the team and said, "Did Michael Jordan ever quit?" The team responded, "No!" He yelled, "What about the Wright brothers? Did they ever give up?" "No!" hollered back the team. "Did

Muhammad Ali ever quit?" Again the team yelled, "No!" "Did Elmer McAllister ever quit?"

There was a long silence. Finally one player was bold enough to ask, "Who's Elmer McAllister? We've never heard of him." The coach snapped back, "Of course you've never heard of him—he quit!"

As you can see, it's important to never give up. I remember a young jockey who lost his first race, his second, his third, his first 10, his first 20, then it became 200, and 250. Finally, Eddie Arcaro won his first race and went on to become one of the all-time great jockeys.

Even Babe Ruth, considered by sports historians to be the greatest baseball player of all time, failed on many occasions. He struck out 1,330 times.

Sir Winston Churchill, himself a person who never quit in a lifetime of defeats and setbacks, delivered the shortest and most eloquent commencement address ever given. Despite taking three years to get through eighth grade because of his trouble learning English grammar, Churchill was asked to address the graduates of Oxford University. As he approached the podium with his trademark cigar, cane, and top hat, he shouted, "Never give up!" Several seconds passed before he rose to his toes and repeated, "Never, never give up." Then he sat down.

MACKAY'S MORAL:

Big shots are only little shots who keep shooting.

Avoid These or It's Return to Sender

Chapter 17

DON'T GET CLOCKED

We save it. We shave it. But we can't store it, speed it up, or slow it down. It's the same for all of us.

Time.

I learned time management skills at a ripe young age by following my Associated Press correspondent–father around. He lived by deadlines. And aphorisms. "Miss a deadline, miss a headline." "Time is the only thing you've got as much of to spend every day as any Rockefeller."

When Jack Mackay said to his 10-year-old fishing partner, "Be at the dock at 2:13," there was no built-in fudge factor. If you got there at 2:14, you were holding your fishing pole in one hand and waving bon voyage with the other. Tough love, kid, but it worked.

My first job after I graduated from college was with Brown & Bigelow. They made advertising and promotional novelties, like calendars and playing cards. I was in the executive training program . . . I pushed a broom in the factory.

When the realization dawned that my future at B&B didn't extend beyond the handle of my broom, I left, and got the second and last job of my life. Selling envelopes. Not wanting to return to broomwork, I asked my father for some career advice.

"What do you want to accomplish?" he asked.

My dream was to make twice as much money as my fellow envelope salespeople had made their first year of selling.

"How many sales calls are you going to make in the next 12 months?"

Hmmm. My peers made about five calls a day. I didn't see any reason why I couldn't match them call for call. "No good," he said. "Do what they do and you'll make what they make. The answer's easy. Figure out how you can make 10 calls a day and your income will double." So we figured it out. We worked out a game plan. It turned out to be a life plan.

- I poked around and learned that some of the buyers' working hours were not the usual 9 to 5 of the typical envelope flogger. Some buyers came in at 6 A.M. Some worked until 7 P.M. Some came in Saturday mornings. For three hours every morning, two hours every afternoon, and four hours on Saturday, I had no competition. Naturally, this turned out to be my most productive time, not the so-called normal hours when all the cookie-cutter-type salespeople were banging into each other. I called them the "Golden Hours."

- I stopped making cold calls. I called ahead to make sure the buyer was in . . . and that I had an appointment. That rather elementary gambit also carried a small, but subtle message. If my time was sufficiently valuable so that I didn't care to spend it cruising around town waiting for a buyer to spare me a few precious moments, then perhaps the product I was selling was valuable, too.

- I was the first kid on my block to get a car phone. Driving is every salesperson's number one time waster. I'll do anything to make the time more productive. Most of the chapters you read here were first spouted into a tape recorder as the telephone poles whizzed by. Also, I'm a freak for cassette tapes. Sometimes, when there's a book I'm really interested in, I'll use the double-barreled approach. I buy the book and I buy the tape of the author reading the book. When it's windshield time, I listen. When it's down time, I read.

(If you're interested in building an audio-tape library, here's the telephone number that can change your life: 800-525-9000. That's Nightingale Conant Company in the Chicago area. They're the biggest and the best.)

- No parking lots for me. Yes, valet parking costs more. But figure it out. Is the two bucks you save worth the 10 minutes you lose?

- Telephone tag is the number two time waster. I never leave my name for a return phone call without a designated time I can be reached. It's another pointed reminder that I'm a busy guy, too, and I don't care to squander my time any more than the buyer cares to squander his or hers.

- Ah, those magic moments swapping war stories with the bull-pen gang. Forget it. Another wasted hour every morning. When was the last time you got an order from another salesperson? Start your day with coffee with a customer.

- Some people love to waste time. Some of them are in your life. If they work for you, ask them to report to you in writing. Tell them you heard that when Dwight Eisenhower was president, he insisted that any memo be limited to a single page. If he could run the country that way, you'd like to see if you could run your little corner of the world the same way. If you have to meet with a time waster, schedule it shortly before *they* have to leave the building.

MACKAY'S MORAL:

Time is precious. You can't own it, but you can use it. You can't keep it, but you can spend it. Once you've lost it, you can never get it back.

Chapter 18

NOT EXACTLY CHOPPED LIVER

Years ago, before he went into private practice and made a bundle, Pat was the city attorney. One day, the city auditor, Edgar, who was running for reelection in six weeks, rushed into Pat's office and told him that he thought he had caught Sol, a city planner, cheating on his expense account. The city was considering helping to finance a new sports arena and the city council had sent Sol and a couple of other planners to the big-league cities around the country to check out their new stadiums.

"Have we caught him?" asked Edgar.

"I dunno," answered Pat. "What makes you think so?"

"These separate tabs for his meals. He's got a separate voucher for every single meal for 16 days. Have we got him?"

"I dunno!"

"Every meal? No one else is asking to be reimbursed for every meal. Have we got him?"

"I dunno."

"Look at this, will ya, Pat? I happen to know that meals were included as part of a package deal when we booked the rooms these guys were staying in. Sol didn't eat a single one of those meals. This guy's receipts are all off the charts. Now, dammit, have we got him?"

"No, Edgar, not if Sol ate kosher."

Does your company have an Edgar? You know Edgar, he's the guy from accounting whose life's work is to make things as miserable as possible for anyone with an expense account, particularly salespeople. Edgar is the guy with the pocket protector, arm bands, and the perpetual scowl on his face. He wears both a belt and suspenders. He's not taking any chances.

Your company may be on-line, paperless, have the most up-to-date technology there is, but Edgar doesn't care. He has the Edgar System. You have to handwrite the forms, attach receipts for everything over $2.98, and have three copies, signed off by your boss and your boss's boss. Edgar's only concession to the dawning of the twenty-first century is his use of Post-it notes. He slaps them on the vouchers he returns, with "Not approved" written on them.

Every company's Edgar is a little different from the next, but they all have one thing in common. The only thing they love more than paperwork is the opportunity to bounce a salesperson's voucher.

Salespeople are hired to sell, not to spend their time going to meetings, tidying up their workspace, or wrangling over paperwork. However, having spent a lifetime running afoul of the Edgars of the world, I realize they, too, have a place in the Great Scheme of Things.

Salespeople, being salespeople, do need some controls. Many companies have found themselves in serious trouble because they bid on every job, concentrated only on revenue, and didn't keep an eye on expenses.

A modern, up-to-date version of Edgar has a broader perspective than the penny-ante concerns of the Edgars of old. Today's Edgar is a strategic planner who looks over all of the company's business opportunities and helps decide which business is profitable and worth spending serious money to pursue and which business isn't worth bidding on because the margins are too thin. He works with the sales force. He has an input on pricing and expenses *before* they're incurred. That way, both he and the sales force experience fewer surprises when the vouchers start rolling in.

I believe in doing what has to be done to make both Edgar's and the salesperson's job easier—because if they work at cross-purposes, the company won't be profitable, and there won't be jobs for either of them.

For the past 20 years our Edgar at Mackay Envelope Corporation has been Chief Financial Officer Paul Stang, who has no equal in our industry. Our sales force calls him Scrooge but trust me . . . he's a creative Scrooge!

MACKAY'S MORAL:

Salespeople sell and bean counters count. Smart management gets them both on the same team.

Chapter 19

ANOTHER BONEHEAD PLAY

"Peanuts" readers are familiar with the annual episode where Lucy snatches away a football just as Charlie Brown is about to kick it. Each year Lucy assures him that this time it will be different and she will not, cross her heart and hope to die, pull the ball away at the last moment. Each year Charlie Brown believes her and lands on his keister.

My father had his own variation on this theme.

"Son, would you like to learn a lesson that might save your life in business some day?" my father asked me when I was just eight.

"Sure I would, Dad," I answered.

"Just slide down the banister and I'll catch you," he urged.

"But how do I *know* you'll catch me?" I asked.

"Because I'm your father, and I said I would catch you."

I slid. And landed on the carpet. As I dusted myself off, he announced, "Never trust anyone in business; not even your own father. Business is business."

That short, bumpy ride didn't involve any "business" I'd ever heard about, but the lesson stuck anyway. Since then, I've gone to great lengths to make sure that any business arrangement I'm involved in is backed up with yards of paper that describe exactly who does what and what happens if they don't. Understandings prevent misunderstandings. Banisters are great teaching devices.

But sometimes every pupil needs a refresher course.

Some years ago we held a series of corporate planning sessions at Mackay Envelope Corporation. We decided we needed additional capacity both in machinery and square footage. My management team strongly suggested we build out of town and in Iowa for two main reasons: (1) we were sole suppliers to many major accounts and couldn't take a chance on a work stoppage, and (2) southeast Iowa is a lot closer to Chicago than Minneapolis and if we were ever going to crack that market, we needed to lower freight costs.

So what did I do?

I decided to ignore the advice and expand in Minneapolis. Why?

Because I was in line to become president of the Minneapolis Chamber of Commerce and I didn't want to embarrass myself and my board members with an ugly headline in the paper that read: MINNEAPOLIS CHAMBER PRESIDENT MOVES COMPANY TO IOWA.

In other words, I made a decision based solely on emotion and ego, not sound business reasoning. I wanted the approval of my peers. I wanted folks to say, "Harvey, you're a hometown hero."

I made the decision with my heart. And guess what it got me? Two big As: Angst and Angina.

Shortly after we expanded in Minneapolis, we were hit with a 12-week strike, the first shutdown in our 15 years of business. It was devastating. It almost crippled us permanently. Chapter 11 was right around the corner and with it a potential headline even uglier than the one I had been so afraid of, this one reading: MINNEAPOLIS CHAMBER PRESIDENT'S BUSINESS TANKS WHILE HE ENCOURAGES OTHERS TO EXPAND HERE.

Although our flagship plant and main office remain in Minneapolis, we finally did expand into Iowa, where we now have one of the most modern envelope plants in America. We do a thriving business in Chicago because we're close to our new major market. And, of course, our business is more secure for all our employees, both in Minnesota and Iowa, because not all our eggs are in one basket.

We also have a sadder but wiser Mackay.

MACKAY'S MORAL:

Put your own little self aside when you make business decisions or you'll wind up with ego on your face.

Chapter 20

WHEN SMART PEOPLE DO STUPID THINGS

In athletics, as well as business, I've always had a fondness for the gutsy competitor, the type who wouldn't back down from anyone. Pete Rose. Wayne Gretzky. Bobby Knight. George Patton. Vince Lombardi. Frank Sinatra. Lee Iacocca.

All legendary for pushing the envelope. And you know how I feel about envelopes.

There are times, though, when the scalpel works better than the sledgehammer.

I was sitting in the audience at a city council hearing many years ago when the agenda items that preceded my zoning variance were two liquor license violations. Both involved after-hours sales, hardly a great moral issue.

The first bar owner had hired an expensive attorney who seemed more interested in trying to impress his client than the council members, and that's exactly what happened. Flashing gold cufflinks and a matching Rolex, and wearing what looked like a $2,000 suit, he tried to bowl over the council with a lot of legal terminology and thinly veiled threats of lawsuits against the city. The $9,000-a-year council members hated him on sight. What did they care if he sued the city? They weren't personally liable. Result: guilty to the max. The bar's license was suspended for 10 days.

That may not sound like much, but in the saloon business it can be fatal. There's always another bar. It doesn't take long to switch loyalties.

Next case. The second bar owner represented himself. His clothes looked like he'd picked them out that morning from the Salvation Army free bin. In a voice barely above a whisper, he apologized to the distinguished council members. Business had been bad lately, but that was no excuse. He had stepped out of line. He had made a terrible mistake. He realized that his license was a great privilege and he had abused that privilege. He would accept whatever punishment was due him. Only, he just wanted the council to know it would never happen again.

By the time he was finished, the council members looked like they were ready to buy him a drink at his own bar. After hours.

The council let him off with a warning.

At that point I told my lawyer to go back to the office, I'd take it from there.

Whatever you're selling, ya gotta know the territory.

Senator Sam Ervin of North Carolina was the chairman of the Senate Judiciary Committee during the Watergate hearings. The contrast between the shambling, drawling Southerner and the smooth-talking, slicked-back Nixon accomplices, like John Dean and Charles Colson, couldn't have been more vivid.

Ervin liked to describe himself as a "simple country lawyer." A more accurate description would be "a super-smart Harvard Law School graduate who lulled his opponents into underestimating his ability."

Ervin probably did more to bring down the Nixon administration than anyone else.

Jack and Ray both sold envelopes for us. Both were about the same age and had similar backgrounds. The major difference between them was style. Jack had a kind of "ah shucks" manner that put customers at ease.

Ray was more intent on scoring points than on listening to his customers. He had to prove to everyone that he knew more about envelopes than any other human being on the face of the earth. An envelope is an envelope is an envelope. You buy from someone you like. Jack sold a lot more envelopes than Ray did.

The know-it-all invariably has a tough time in sales. Customers tend to get uncomfortable around someone who has all the answers. "If this salesperson knows so much, what does he know that he isn't telling me?"

If you're in sales, it never hurts to tell a customer that you *don't* know the answer to their excellent question, but you'll check it out and give them a call . . . pronto.

Customers don't expect you to know everything.

They will respect you more when they see you won't just wing it and tell them what they want to hear.

And—not the least of the advantages to this approach—you will have a legitimate reason to make a follow-up call.

Mackay's Moral:

Some people are too smart for their own good. But they're not smart enough to know they don't know.

LICKING THE COMPETITION

WHAT EVERY
GOOD STAMP
COLLECTOR KNOWS

Chapter 21

12 WAYS TO RUIN YOUR NEXT SPEECH

In a recent survey of the top 10 fears of Americans, what do you suppose was right at the top of the list? Certainly not death. Death is minor compared to the perennial number one fear in America. Did you guess it? It's public speaking, of course.

When I say that in speeches, everyone laughs. Then they nod.

Why is public speaking so terrifying? It has a lot to do with feeling exposed. We're terrified of looking stupid or having something go wrong while we're up there, all alone. Luckily, millions of dollars have been spent over the years on speechwriters, speech coaches, and technology experts who have taken the terror of the unknown out of the speaking experience. Right?

Wrong.

Regardless of the huge investments made in making public speaking a more hazard-free experience, the number of things that can go wrong is still pretty close to infinite. During my speaking career, I've experienced fire drills, building evacuations, power outages, medical emergencies, burst water pipes . . . you name it, it's happened. And a lot of what happens will be beyond your control. Your job is to manage the factors you can control by challenging the 12 lethal assumptions that lead an innocent and well-intentioned speaker to the gallows. Here they are:

1. They've finally managed to make microphones that work.
Unfortunately modern science does not confirm this innocent assumption. True, microphones work better than they used to,

about 80 percent of the time. Not bad, but how would you feel about air travel if it worked about 80 percent of the time? The solution: make sure you have a backup mike (with new batteries), and see to it that whoever is responsible for making the sound system work is in the room when you speak.

2. Just ignore that noise coming from the room next door.
Virtually every hotel in America has a runway or kitchen adjacent to one of the walls in your meeting room and it's an automatic speech killer. Meet with the hotel or catering staff and insist on no table clearing, kitchen noise, next-door activity, *no action whatsoever,* while you speak. Your goal is to be able to hear a pin drop.

3. Dim the lights. That quiet, restful atmosphere will help the audience concentrate.
Quiet, restful atmospheres are for sleeping, not speaking. Be sure the lights are turned up as high as they'll go. Audiences remember more in brightness and share laughter much more frequently. I like the feeling of being able to look at my audience and seeing the whites of their eyes. And skip the slides unless they're absolutely necessary. They're another excuse for your audience to snooze.

4. Give your audience plenty of extra space to spread out.
Every speaker must know by now that if you expect 500 people in your audience, you want a room that seats 400. Empty seats announce that what you had to say wasn't worth the effort to show up. The sardine effect commands attention. If you're stuck with a room you can't fill, make sure there are folding screens or planters available to block the view of the empty areas.

5. Don't bother filling the first couple of rows.
Here's a great way to lose touch with your audience. You can just feel your self-confidence ebb as your eyes search the

empty rows, desperate for human contact. Move your audience toward the front by roping off the last third of the room and not opening up these seats until the crowd is bumper to bumper.

6. The occasional clang of huge entry doors adds a festive note to your remarks.

I may be the only guy in the world who carries a roll of masking tape in my briefcase. Just nail down that latch and voilà, you have noiseless doors.

7. Make sure there's plenty of aisle space in your room.

Make sure there isn't. Direct the staff to put the seats as close together as the fire marshal will allow. Crowds generate enthusiasm.

8. When you're addressing a luncheon or dinner meeting, don't bother about giving the people with their backs to you a chance to turn their chairs around.

The only creature with the ability to rotate its head 180 degrees is a barn owl. Have your introducer invite everyone to face the podium before you get underway.

9. Anyone can handle an introduction.

An introduction is as important to a speaker as a leadoff hitter is to a ball team. Too many groups pick an introducer as a way to confer an honor, not on the basis of talent. With predictable results. Insist on the best-qualified public speaker in the organization.

10. A podium is a podium.

Most podiums and lecterns behave as if they were designed by the same hand as those killer mikes. If the speaker's material can't be seen by the audience, if two legal-sized sheets of paper can't fit side by side, if the angle is so sharp the pages dribble off and flutter to the floor, it's amateur night. Go state of the art. Get a lectern that's automatically adjustable by height and tilt, and has its own self-contained light so you can drive with your brights on and not have to rely on room lighting. A clock staring you in the face will keep you up to speed.

11. At last, it's almost over. Q&A time. Relax and enjoy it.

How many times have you heard a speaker wind up a pretty decent talk, then call for questions, followed by dead silence? The pro makes sure there are several questioners planted in the audience. I didn't say "questions," I said "questioners." Canned exchanges are easy to detect and destroy a speaker's credibility.

Now, the most important idea in this chapter. Start your question and answer session five minutes before the real end of your speech. Never, never end on a Q&A because you want to end with your own "killer close." Trust me, 99.9 percent of speakers never go for the big finish!

12. If you avoid the pitfalls set out in rules 1–11 you've got it made.

I was the keynote speaker in front of 1,000 charged up IBM people and had just gotten rolling when a fire alarm went off. The room emptied in total pandemonium. False alarm, of course. After milling around outside for the next fifteen minutes, we all went back inside. The audience never settled down and I gave the worst speech of my life. Murphy's law was made for moments like this.

MACKAY'S MORAL:

Speeches are like diamonds: no matter how much they seem to sparkle when they're lying on the table, they need the right setting to bring out their best.

P. S. The single best way to enjoy pitfall-free events is to make use of the National Speakers Association. If you want to become a top-flight professional speaker, they're the ones to call. You can reach NSA's headquarters in Tempe, Arizona, at 602-968-2552, or via the Web at www.nsaspeaker.org

Chapter 22

做課外作業

Bob Hope invariably opened his road shows with topical references to his audience and to wherever it was he was performing, be it the 101st Airborne in Korea or the Shriners in Peoria.

It's an old trick, but it always works—if the performer knows his material is right for the audience.

In 1998 I was invited to put on a seminar in Taipei, Taiwan. The host company told me there would be about 3000 Chinese people in attendance and that very few of them knew English. I would have to speak through an interpreter.

As if any audience weren't challenge enough, I knew that even Bob Hope would be hard-pressed to put a joke over if it had to be told through an interpreter. With my favorite opener gone, how was I going to make this work?

I told the company I would come on one condition: I insisted that they arrange to have me there a day early, so I could practice with a representative group—minimum 12 people.

They agreed, and we wound up with a jury panel consisting of a teacher, salesperson, doctor, stockbroker, insurance salesperson, nurse. . . . In other words, the cast of every war picture that has ever been made. "All right, First Platoon, I want 12 volunteers. That'll be O'Malley, Hernandez, Shapiro, Jackson. . . ."

I needed to make sure my anecdotes, examples, stories, aphorisms, and yes, gulp, even jokes, if I could get away with any, would be clearly understood and not culturally incorrect.

After the first run-through with the group I threw away 30 percent of my material.

Second run-through, another 15 percent hit the fan.

Third run-through, 5 percent more.

Fourth run-through, all systems go.

It took four test flights and six hours before I had a two-hour presentation that I knew would work, top to bottom. And knowing gave me the added confidence to put it over that much more effectively.

Another bit of extra effort that really paid off was to work with Berlitz International—a language center with offices throughout the United States and in 32 countries—until I was able to deliver the first 10 minutes of my pitch in Mandarin Chinese. During the all-important 10-minute opener, I had my translator interpret my Mandarin back to the audience in English—which no one understood—and it got a respectable chuckle. Hey, I'm no Bob Hope.

MACKAY'S MORAL:

Oh yes, that headline. It's "Do Your Homework" in Mandarin Chinese.

Chapter 23

PHOTO OP

Are there any heights to which mankind can aspire that can be denied a humble envelope man?

No, not me. I'm not that humble.

Dick Berkley.

Dick served 12 years (1979–1991) as mayor of Kansas City.

Dick also is an owner of Tension Envelope, one of the largest nationwide envelope manufacturers.

Did he slip the voters an envelope or two on election day? "Hey, pal, vote for me and this #10 is yours to keep." No, let's face it, not even Ken Starr would be impressed with a free envelope.

Dick leveraged his favorite hobby, photography, and built a political base at the same time.

He has always carried a state-of-the-art camera small enough to fit into his shirt pocket. At the airport, attending the symphony ball, chamber of commerce luncheon, doing whatever it is a mayor does, Mayor Berkley will click on in seconds and your picture is mailed to you promptly with a little personalized note on it.

Over the years I think Dick has taken more pictures of me than my mother did. In his most recent, he didn't even need me to be there. It was a photo of the cover of my latest book, sitting on a Barnes and Noble shelf in Los Angeles. Dick's signature Post-it note was on the photo, reading: "Would you buy a used car from this man?" Dick, though somewhat artistically challenged, had even gone to the trouble of drawing two check-off boxes beneath the question. A "Yes" box and a "No" box. He had checked the "No" box. What a touching sentiment. Typical envelope guy.

Dick Berkley, grand master networker, had struck again. Here's a communication that goes up on the office bulletin board and then retires to a permanent place in the scrapbook.

MACKAY'S MORAL:

Warm, personal note to Dick Berkley: America needs your people skills and creativity. Go back into politics. I don't need the competition.

Chapter 24

TELEPHONE 101

My father taught me how to ride a bike. My mother taught me how to read. My high school typing teacher taught me how to type. My tennis instructor taught me . . . well, I'm still taking lessons. Some things you have to keep learning your whole life.

Like how to use a phone. It's too bad none of us can remember who taught us that. Because if we did, maybe we wouldn't take telephones so much for granted. Your business is on the receiving end of countless phone calls every day, many of them from customers and prospects. The first impression these people have of your company is the voice on the receiving end of your phone.

If that voice belongs to a computer-generated receiving device rather than a real live human being, listen up to this cautionary tale.

Jerry started reading a new business magazine. He thought that it was one terrific magazine and he read every issue cover to cover. When he decided to subscribe, he wanted it to start immediately so he didn't miss a single issue. Inside the magazine there were lots of blow-in coupons offering subscription deals, but he didn't want to have to fill out a coupon and mail it in and wait six weeks for his subscription to kick in.

There was no phone number listed on the coupon that he could call to subscribe. That should have been the tip-off that this outfit did not want to do business with him the way he wanted to do business. But Jerry figured that, as a customer, there should be a way for him to subscribe that was convenient for him. So he looked on the masthead of the magazine. There in tiny type was an 800 number for subscription services. Jerry called. A computer-activated answering device played a message saying "your call is very important to us," and then put him on hold for 10 minutes. Jerry hung up. He called back later and got a new message. The new message said that because office hours were from 9 A.M. to 5:30 P.M., the office was now closed. It was 5:15 P.M.

There was, however, a tiny little ray of sunshine at the end of the magazine's recorded message. Jerry could, if he wished, leave his own message. He did. He concluded by asking how it was that a magazine with the word "business" in its title didn't know enough about "business" to make it convenient for their customers to do "business" with them? He didn't subscribe either. He found he was able to live without the magazine after all.

If you think having a machine answer your phones is a great technological advance with a positive impact on your bottom line, then I have a suggestion for you: Fire all your salespeople and have a machine sell all your goods or services. I guarantee that will save you even more money. However, I can't say what it will do for your sales.

How your telephone is answered says more about your company than all your slick advertising and marketing plans can ever hope to accomplish.

Your telephone receptionist is the most important salesperson in your company. Notice I said "person," not "tool" or "device."

At Mackay Envelope Corporation, I always do the hiring for just two slots: president and telephone receptionist. If whoever answers those phone calls does not have a warm, helpful, outgoing personality and does not have professional training, you are missing your single best, most cost-effective means for improving your bottom line.

Call Mackay Envelope and Tamara VanGuilder will answer the phone in three to four rings. Her voice will be pleasant because there's always a smile on her face. When you have become a regular caller, chances are Tamara will recognize you and call you by name before you announce yourself.

I know that our Mackay envelopes are better than anyone else's because they are delivered on time, with value received, and we very seldom lose any customers. But I also can tell you two things about us for sure: We have the best telephone receptionist in the country, and business is terrific.

> ## MACKAY'S MORAL:
>
> Show me a good phone receptionist and I'll show
> you a good company.

Chapter 25

TAKE YOUR WORK SERIOUSLY, DON'T TAKE YOURSELF SERIOUSLY

"Dilbert," which is carried in 1,100 newspapers, has helped us laugh at the crazy dynamics of the workplace. Now if we could only start laughing at ourselves.

The late and much beloved chief executive of Coca-Cola, Roberto Goizueta, had the ability. He could distance himself from a situation, and by standing back and observing things objectively, he could see the irony. It's no accident the market value of Coke in 16 years increased from $4 billion to $145 billion. Humor is a critical business weapon.

In the midst of the New Coke debacle in the 1980s, conspiracy buffs circulated the idea that Coca-Cola introduced this "mistake" deliberately to get more attention for Coke. When presented with that theory, Goizueta answered that Coke was neither smart enough nor dumb enough to have dreamed up the ploy.

On the other hand, we've all worked for the humorless. There are the bosses whom I call "Rocky" who take on the whole world through earnestness. And we're in big trouble if we don't seem equally serious. We can't joke that sales plunged one percent or that a supplier might not meet a deadline. In such offices you can cut the tension with a knife. And usually results aren't what they could be.

No matter who's the boss, we can still get a few laughs at our own expense—and be able to work better. A colleague of mine is a genius at this. If his plane is late and his blood pressure is rising, he distances himself. He often thinks to himself: "How will this 'nightmare' seem to me a year from now . . . a blip on the screen?" In his mind's eye he can see that it was just a brief scene in this saga we call "life." Another colleague, when stressed out, tries to imagine how he would explain his "predicament" to his six-year-old. Pretty quickly the concerns of the day start to sound ridiculous. He calls that "baby-proofing" his consciousness.

There's no excuse for total, self-absorbed seriousness. It's boring. It pushes others away from you. And it requires a whole lot of energy to assume such a world view. Oh, of course, there are times for seriousness. But we all know when they are. If the company can't seem to achieve a turnaround there will be plenty of people focused solely on the bottom line. No chuckles there. When someone else has a problem, it's showing respect to treat their situation seriously. In addition, as we enter a company or grow into a new job, we can leave the levity to others. At my company there are few managers-in-training who are a barrel of laughs. Learning the ropes is definitely serious business.

On formal performance appraisals, it might be a good idea if we introduced the category "Can laugh at themselves." In an organization where a little self-deprecation is encouraged, people are more likely to take risks and therefore make mistakes. In the current global marketplace, where there are few precedents anymore, plenty of errors of judgment are going to be made.

Incidentally, Coca-Cola eventually hired back the man who put New Coke on the market. Those who can't laugh at themselves should be penalized. Their overearnestness can be an albatross around the neck of the organization.

MACKAY'S MORAL:

Lighten up.

WITH THE RIGHT SPIN, A TWO-CENT STAMP CAN BE WORTH MILLIONS

Chapter 26

HOW TO
GET A RAISE

If you're an active investor, you probably keep a close eye on the Federal Reserve. The Fed regulates monetary policy, raising interest rates when the indicators suggest inflationary pressures, lowering them to encourage borrowing when the economy has slowed.

The late William McChesney Martin, Fed chairman during the go-go '60s, once said he was responsible for taking away the punch bowl before the party got too wild.

Despite a booming economy, many sophisticated analysts believe that the Fed is keeping its hands off the punch bowl. It won't tighten much further, because even though unemployment is low, another key indicator, wage rates, have remained relatively flat.

Some economists attribute these stagnant wage levels to increasing productivity.

I attribute them to the Rickey/Mayer syndrome, a little-known economic theory that, casting aside false modesty, I must admit to having thought up myself. I'm still working out the equations. Right now, the R/M theory is purely anecdotal. Let me share my research with you.

In 1947 Branch Rickey was the man who made the first unheard-of move to put a black man, Jackie Robinson, in a Brooklyn Dodger uniform. That wasn't the only reason he was one of the greatest general managers who ever lived. He got more for less than any boss in history. Gene Hermanski was an outfielder with the Dodgers. This was the pre–Jerry Maguire era when ballplayers negotiated their own contracts. "I had a great year, and I'm going to demand a $10,000 raise," said Hermanski to the press outside Rickey's office as he marched in for his annual session with "The Mahatma." He was in with Rickey a long time. When he came out the reporters mobbed him.

"Did you get the raise?"

"No, but I didn't get a cut either."

Louis B. Mayer, the head of MGM many years ago, was another boss who had the reputation of throwing nickels around like they were manhole covers. He could also shed more crocodile tears than the legendary actress Sarah Bernhardt. Matinee idol Robert Taylor was grossly underpaid and made an appointment to see Mayer and insist on a raise. Before Taylor could make his pitch, Mayer began talking.

"Bob, I'm so glad to see you. There's something I've been wanting to tell you. As you know, the Lord has blessed me with two lovely children. They happen to be daughters, but who's complaining? It's just that if I ever were to have a son"—by this time tears were streaming down Mayer's cheeks—"I'd want him to be just like you. As loyal, as kind, as understanding, as selfless and giving and caring as Robert Taylor. Now what is it you wanted to see me about . . . Son?"

When Taylor left the office, his agent was waiting.

"Did you get a raise?"

"No, but I got a father."

The downsizing of corporate America has created regiments of little Rickey/Mayers, skilled and determined to hold down costs at all costs.

I'm an employer, and if I had half a brain I wouldn't be sharing this information, but with an economy that is very, very strong, and workers in great demand, you don't have to go hat in hand when you ask for a raise these days.

The number one rule is "be prepared." The game plan. The

backup plan. The responses to objections. Negotiating is selling. Prepare a sales pitch.

- Research your target. Pick your time carefully. When you asked Dad for the car keys, did you hit him when he walked in the door or wait until after he'd had his dinner and was in a good mood?
- Know the company. What percentage did profits, sales, and market share increase last year?
- Know the competition. What are other people at other companies getting paid for your slot? This is particularly useful when you haven't been all that productive. You still might be able to demonstrate that you're underpaid.
- Know your product. That's you. Keep a log of your accomplishments. Write it down. Make notes in your daily calendar. That way, you won't forget anything, and you'll have the most valuable form of proof there is: written evidence.
- If you get turned down, set the table for the next round. Ask: "What do I have to do in the next 6 to 12 months to accomplish my economic goals?"
- Don't threaten. Don't bluff. Don't be afraid to ask.

MACKAY'S MORAL:

If you want them to show you the money, you better
show them the reason.

Chapter 27

LET'S MAKE
A DEAL

I got a phone call from a Fortune 500 CEO recently whom I had never met. After decades of begging the government to relax their regulatory grip and let his industry experience the joys of competition, his wish had been granted—and his bottom line had plummeted.

He wanted me to talk to his top executives for two hours and zero in on negotiating strategies.

A bit overwhelmed, I said, "I'm very flattered but frankly, I don't know if I can talk for two hours on negotiating."

Then I realized I was actually negotiating with myself. As my brain finally reconnected, I cut myself off.

"Well, let me sleep on it and I'll get back to you."

Later that evening I began to write down some of my negotiating experiences and saw that my problem was going to be holding the speech down to two hours.

I'd already brushed up against the first and second laws of negotiating that morning in my conversation with the CEO:

1. Never accept any proposal immediately, no matter how good it sounds.
2. Never negotiate with yourself. Once you've made an offer, if the other party doesn't accept it, don't make another offer. Get a counteroffer. It's a sign of weakness when you lower your own demands without getting your opponent to lower theirs.

Here are some more rules of the road:

3. Never cut a deal with someone who has to "go back and get the boss's approval." That gives the other side two bites of the apple to your one. They can take any deal you are willing to make and renegotiate it.
4. If you can't say yes, it's no. Just because a deal can be done, doesn't mean it *should* be done. No one ever went broke saying no too often.
5. Just because it may look nonnegotiable, doesn't mean it is. Take that beautifully printed "standard contract" you've just been handed. Many a smart negotiator has been able to name a term and get away with it by making it appear to be chiseled in granite, when, in fact, they would deal if their bluff were called.
6. Do your homework before you deal. Learn as much as you can about the other side. Instincts are no match for information.
7. Rehearse. Practice. Get someone to play the other side. Then switch roles. Instincts are no match for preparation.
8. Beware the late dealer. Feigning indifference or casually disregarding timetables is often just a negotiator's way of trying to make you believe he/she doesn't care if you make the deal or not.
9. Be nice, but if you can't be nice, or if you're too nice, go away and let someone else do the deal. You'll blow it.
10. A deal can always be made when both parties see their own benefit in making it.
11. A dream is a bargain no matter what you pay for it. Set the scene. Tell the tale. Generate excitement. Help the other side visualize the benefits, and they'll sell themselves.
12. Watch the game films. Top players in any game, including negotiating, debrief themselves immediately after every major session. They always keep a book on themselves and the other side.

13. No one is going to show you their hole card. You have to figure out what they really want. Clue: Since the given reason is never the real reason, you can eliminate the given reason.
14. Always let the other side talk first. Their first offer could surprise you and be better than you ever expected.

MACKAY'S MORAL:

Gambits are to negotiation what notes are to music:
If you want to carry a tune, you better learn the scales.

Chapter 28

LET'S MAKE
A DEAL II

Like war, the winner in a business negotiation is not necessarily the side that has the most firepower. It is the side that has the most information about its opponents and applies whatever leverage it has to the weakest point in their defense.

Here are some more common sense tips that you can apply to any negotiation:

- Don't get personal. That attitude has a higher kill ratio than Black Talon bullets. You don't have to like your opponent, but don't let your dislike become obvious. There is no reason to make your competition choose between self-respect and self-interest in order to deal with you.

- Don't show your emotions. Bluster is a sign of weakness, not strength. Keep a poker face, particularly if you think you came out a winner. You may have to go back to the table again someday with the same opponents. Whom would you rather sit down with: someone who wants to deal, or someone who wants to get even?

- Don't talk out of school. If you discuss your deals in elevators, you have definitely pushed the "down" button. It's a small world . . . and the walls have ears.

- Leave something on the table for the other guy. Peace treaties are made between enemies, not friends, but it usually takes a war to get them to the bargaining table. Deals are made between parties who seek mutual advantage, not unilateral victory. Both sides have to win something, or you don't have a deal, you have a homicide. One way or another, your competitor will see to it that crime doesn't pay.

- Your first offer should never be your final offer. Don't create a situation where your opponent can't justify his value to his principal by accepting your offer. Give the person on the other side of the table a chance to knock you down a little. Remember the previous point: they need to win something, too.

- Don't be afraid to take a risk. The trial lawyer who says he or she never lost a case settles too easily. Don't let yourself be bluffed by artificial deadlines or "final offers." And don't run bluffs either. If you are called and you don't follow through, your credibility is shot.

- Don't be afraid to go to an expert when you're in over your head. You don't know everything. Trying to pretend to your opponent, your client, or yourself that you are knowledgeable in some area or have some vital information when you don't, harms your position. It makes you appear weak and foolish in the eyes of your opponent.

- Don't attribute more strength to the other side than they possess. This is classic Von Clausewitz. Every opponent has weaknesses. In any negotiation, *both* sides are under pressure to perform. They have bosses, stresses, fears, and objectives, just like you do.

- Sometimes you can get what you want by calling it by another name. Let's say your opponent does not "renegotiate" contracts. Okay, what if we call it a contract "extension"? Your opponent says no to severance pay? Okay, it's a consulting contract. A potential employer does not want to hire you on a permanent basis? Okay, it's an internship. And you'll work for nothing. They only have to pay you if they care to.

- Take your time. Don't let the other side force a deal. The more time you give yourself, the more information you can gather about your adversary's true needs.

MACKAY'S MORAL:

The best negotiators have iron backsides. They know how to wait until it is in their interest, and not the other side's, to deal. The smartest response you can make to any offer is, "Let me give it some thought."

Chapter 29

MASTERS OF
THE GAME

If I were to ask you "Who is the greatest salesperson of all time?" what would your answer be? It might be a spiritual leader, a person who is able to persuade us to accept on faith something we cannot see, hear, or touch. It could be a coach, someone who can coax us into exerting a superhuman effort or enduring physical pain in hopes of achieving a victory that could fade as quickly as today's headlines. Or a military superior who can inspire us to lay down our lives for our country.

They're all worthy candidates for the title, but I submit that the best salesperson of the bunch is the unworthiest: the successful con artist.

The spiritual leader, the coach, and the commander are dealing in something that, even though it may not be tangible, at least appeals to our desire to appear virtuous and has some basis in truth. A con artist convinces us to reject everything we've been taught to believe in and sells us the oldest and most transparent of all lies: that he can get us something for nothing.

The common misconception is that con artists work on the periphery of society, preying on the most vulnerable.

"How could anyone be so stupid as to fall for that ancient ruse?" we ask ourselves as we read in the paper about some elderly pensioners who lost their life savings in the "pigeon drop."

Then we turn the page to check the lottery results. Every day millions and millions of us supposedly intelligent and sophisticated types, folks who would never fall for a Ponzi scheme, participate in a game that we think pays off winners at 100 to 1 (four out of six numbers), when the true odds are over 6,000 to 1. That's not gambling. That's a con game. Even winners are losers in a game where the house skims $59/60$ of the pot. Your odds are better in a chain letter.

New games keep popping up. The Foundation for A New Era scam is a real doozy.

The con artist at this outfit claimed to represent a group of wealthy philanthropists who didn't want to be identified. He told his victims that his anonymous angels would match any charitable contribution they made. It seems ridiculous that anyone would believe this without convincing evidence, but among the people who did were some of the most savvy investors and entrepreneurs in the world. According to *Time* magazine, the group included Laurance S. Rockefeller; William F. Simon; John C. Whitehead, former deputy secretary of state; John Pepper, president of Procter & Gamble; Thomas L. Phillips, director of Raytheon; and Lewis Bernard, director of Morgan Stanley Group.

Give these people credit—they were not motivated by personal greed. But that does not excuse them from culpability in their own victimization. They fell for the same line that every pigeon-drop dupe bites on: Give us your money, and you will get unbelievable returns on it.

Whether you're being conned out of your nest egg or your spare change, whether the game is a classic Ponzi scheme, the "Spanish prisoner" ruse, a chain letter, or a pigeon drop, the common denominator for a scam remains the same: something for nothing. And so does the way to spot one: If it sounds too good to be true, it is.

Why did the New Era donors get hooked? Because the con artist was one of their own, a Philadelphia Mainliner who traveled in the same social and business circles as they did. They assumed that because someone lived among them and looked, dressed, acted as they did, he could be trusted.

It isn't the guy you never met before who offers you the business opportunity of a lifetime that you have to worry about.

It's the guy who has the locker next to yours at the country club who makes the same kind of offer.

MACKAY'S MORAL:

Con artists do not wear signs that say CON ARTIST.

Chapter 30

BIDDING WARS

The most exciting moment at an auction is when a spirited bidding war breaks out.

Someone wins. Someone loses. Right?

Wrong.

Put aside the obvious auction scams of rigged bids and phony sales, where the winners are the losers and the losers are the winners. Let's examine the somewhat kinder, gentler milieu of the charity auction, where everyone can wind up a winner.

The genius of this enterprise is a guy named Jimmy Walker, who dreamed up the concept of holding a "Fight Night" as a fund-raiser for Muhammad Ali's Parkinson's Center in Phoenix.

Jimmy rented the ballroom of the best hotel in town, put up a full-size boxing ring, scaled the house for all-ringside tables, black tie only (just 500, so demand exceeded supply . . . Marketing 101), and sprinkled local and national celebrities through the tables . . . Kenny Rogers, Troy Aikman, Paula Abdul, Lou Gossett Jr., Sugar Ray Leonard, Barry Manilow, Mark McGwire, and of course, at table #1, Muhammad Ali.

Now for the fight card. Let's get ready to rumble.

In this corner, straight from the eighth at Turf Paradise, standing five foot four inches and weighing 110 pounds, one of the track's leading jockeys. His opponent, just off the hardwood, standing six foot eleven and three-quarters inches and weighing 280 pounds and 4 ounces, an NBA starting center.

Touch 'em up.

The gloves are bigger than the jockey, but he manages to land a vicious blow to his opponent's kneecap.

I mean, I've heard of below the belt, but below the trunks? The ref misses it completely. He's putting a move on the round-card lady in the bikini. The center comes crashing down like a 2,000-year-old redwood.

"One . . . two . . . ten . . . Y'er out." (What happened to three, four, five, six, seven, eight, and nine?)

Next on the card . . .

One of the celebs gets into the ring. His ring attire consists of boxing shorts about six sizes too big with gloves to match. He manages to throw a tremendous punch. It's a knockout. Himself.

When the show is over, with everyone in a good mood, the live auction begins.

It's the usual trips, condos, tickets, dinner with the celebrities, and the star attraction, Ali, takes a bow. The lights dim. The featured entry is about to go on the block.

The professional auctioneer has the round-card lady circle the ring three times holding up an oversized painting of Ali at the height of his career, done by a well known sports artist. Oohs and aahs.

"Do I hear $2,500?" Several hands go up.

"$5,000?" More hands.

"$7,500?" Yes.

"$10,000?" Yes.

"$12,500?" You got it.

"$15,000?" A big hand waves in the air for the first time. It's Jerry Colangelo, owner and CEO of the Phoenix Suns and the Arizona Diamondbacks.

"$20,000?" Someone tops Colangelo.

"$22,000?" The auctioneer looks at Colangelo. Colangelo nods approval.

"$24,000?" A new player enters the bidding.

"$26,000?" The auctioneer looks at Colangelo. He smiles and folds his hands . . . across his chest.

They continue to move up by $2,000 increments until they

reach $78,000, the high bid, edging out a second-place bid of $76,000.

The place was buzzing. Was this Monopoly money? I leaned over the table to Jimmy Walker. I had an idea.

"Why don't you see if the artist will do another and have the auctioneer ask the number two bidder if he'll pay the seventy-six for the painting?"

Jimmy speaks with the artist, who makes a little okay sign. Then Jimmy motions to the auctioneer and whispers in his ear. The auctioneer goes back to the center of the ring.

"Sir, we don't want anyone to leave this room disappointed. Our distinguished artist says he thinks we can meet your need for the agreed-upon price of $76,000. It may turn out even better the second time around. What do you say?"

What could he say? He was willing to pay $76,000 thirty seconds earlier. No way he could change his mind. Done deal.

The dinner netted a whopping $500,000 for a good cause. As I was leaving, I felt a big paw on my arm. It was Ali. "You devil," he said. "You're worse than Frazier. Did you ever do any fighting?"

MACKAY'S MORAL:

Sometimes you're allowed to throw a punch a teeny bit below the belt when it's for a good cause.

Chapter 31

THE REAL MASTER OF THE GAME

The late Steve Ross was the master of the game. He's the guy they named the book after. Ross clawed his way out of a threadbare Depression boyhood in Brooklyn to become head of Time Warner, the world's largest media and entertainment conglomerate. The story of his rise is told in *Master of the Game*, by Connie Bruck.

Ross concealed a highly acquisitive and competitive nature behind a dazzling facade of charm, opulence, and generosity. Though Ross lived like a Roman emperor, he never lost the common touch. What would start out as a routine walk through the corporate offices would turn into a love-in/pep rally, with Ross stopping to chat it up with every secretary and file clerk along the way, followed the next day with flowers and gifts. He was a visionary who saw the potential of cable television and the combination of cable with movies, music, games, and interactive software as the future of the entertainment business.

And, he was a master deal maker. No one, ever, has matched his ability to read the other side's cards. Having read them, he knew how to play the hand for maximum advantage. He could make his negotiating opponents believe that he, Steve Ross, would fulfill their deepest desires, while at the same time extracting exactly what he wanted for himself out of the negotiation.

How did he do it?

It didn't hurt that despite an indifferent education, Ross had taught himself to read a legal document like a lawyer with a CPA degree, and could multiply one three digit figure by another in his head.

As a child Ross listened to weather reports on the radio, so he could set his alarm for 4 A.M. if it was going to snow. That way he could get the jump on the other kids for the job of shoveling out the driveways of the rich folks' houses.

Ross could overwhelm the most jaded Hollywood type with extravagant gestures, like sending the corporate jet cross-country to pick up Steven Spielberg's dogs so they could join the director on a weekend vacation. Barbra Streisand mentioned to Ross casually how much she regretted having underbid on a sculpture at an auction. Ross tracked down the sculpture, bought it, and gave it to her. Spielberg and Streisand were both drawn into Ross's orbit and both became useful—and profitable—allies in Ross's business dealings.

Seduction of the innocent, and not so innocent, by smothering them with gifts and attention was Ross's trademark negotiating technique. But his own favorite story involved a different approach. As a young man, Ross's first significant managerial job was running his father-in-law's funeral business in New York City. Ross had just bought a site for a new funeral chapel when he learned that Lincoln Center was to be constructed across the street. Ross saw what was coming next, a terrific opportunity to squeeze the uptown swells who would not welcome an endless procession of hearses and mourners across from their elegant new cultural facility. Sure enough a call came from Governor Nelson Rockefeller. Was Ross planning to build a funeral parlor on his land?

Yes.

The governor then asked Ross if he had gotten approval from the zoning commission.

Yes.

"Have you checked that?" the governor asked.

Yes.

"No," said the governor. "I mean, have you checked that *tomorrow?*"

Ross loved to tell that story on himself, probably because there was a happy ending for Ross. Rockefeller eventually sent an underling to negotiate the purchase of Ross's property. The agent's original offer, an oddball number, led Ross to think it was a fraction, like three-quarters, of what he was really willing to pay. So Ross walked.

A few days later, Rockefeller's agent called and made a second, higher offer, another weird figure, and Ross again demurred.

This kept going on until the agent finally reached a figure six times his original offer and over eight times what Ross had paid. The deal was made.

The lesson here was a real-life example of one you've heard me harp on before: Never negotiate with yourself. Once an offer is made, no new offer should be forthcoming until and unless the other side counteroffers. The only exception is when the offeror, hearing no counter, withdraws his original offer and comes back with a *lower* offer.

If Ross had a weakness as a businessperson, it was the typical entrepreneur's unwillingness to sell assets. He rode Atari up, but he rode it down, too. That never would have happened to an Irwin Jacobs, who you heard about in chapter 6. Jacobs's great strength is knowing when to sell. He never falls in love with assets.

I have my own Ross story. I played tennis with him at the John Gardiner Tennis Ranch in Phoenix. Just as Bruck's book tells it, Ross was an intense competitor, though not much of a tennis player. The tip-off came before we even got started. We were playing doubles and spun the racket for partners. He got a partner he didn't want.

"Two out of three," Steve Ross said, turning on his famous 1,000-megawatt grin.

MACKAY'S MORAL:

In negotiations, as in poker, a superior hand can be beaten by superior knowledge of your opponents.

Chapter 32

THE BEST DEAL
I NEVER MADE

The ink wasn't dry on the Citicorp-Travelers deal before the second-guessing began.

Maybe. All I know is that it takes a lot of guts to pull the trigger on any deal. No matter how carefully you think you've checked it out, there are going to be surprises. The word "surprise," in a business context, is *always* modified by the word "unpleasant." The trick is to avoid the mousetraps before they break your neck.

Years ago, I wanted to buy an envelope company in California. I met with the president. He was smart, straight, knowledgeable about his business and its value, and also a seven handicap in golf. Not the least of the attractions of the acquisition—and one my counterpart played like a pro on his home course hustling a visiting duffer—was that my business visits could coincide nicely with the considerable time Minnesota golf courses were under six feet of snow. I spent so much time wandering through the plant, and crawling around the machinery, that one shift asked their union rep to have me thrown out. They thought I was an efficiency expert and a threat to their jobs. They may have been right.

Our accountants met with their accountants. Our lawyers met with their lawyers. We weren't far apart on price. Then, "Surprise!" My golfing partner was no longer the president. He had been offered a chance-of-a-lifetime opportunity with the parent company. With no time to complete our deal, he was on his way to Chicago, where the golf wasn't that great, but the future was.

Suddenly, I had a new negotiating partner. He was an equally good golfer, but he decided to change the rules of the game.

Since the old president was history, the old deal was out. President #2 would show his boss how a real deal should be done. No more mulligans for Harvey.

Scorecards to be checked, verified, and certified after every hole.

He read me right. He knew that I wanted the deal, and not just for a respite from Minnesota winters. We did not have a presence on the West Coast. We needed one.

On the previous round, president #1 had charmed me out of my spikes. Oh, I had done some checking. The company was a major player, aggressive, well managed, well regarded by customers, vendors, and competitors. But I still had not conducted the sort of rigorous due-diligence effort I now put into looking over president #2. I scrutinized him more closely than the Democrats examined Ken Starr's calendar. I even interviewed one of his high school teachers on the phone. He was talented, hard nosed, a careerist who had built his resume jump by jump from one lily pad to the next.

The only trouble was: I didn't like him. He was central to the deal. And as badly as I wanted it, I did not want him running a business for me.

So, it was not California after all. It was el passo.

Two years later he was gone. I took another look at the company in 1991. By this time another new president—this was #3—had taken over. He was a quality professional-numbers man, but not an envelope man. When I went through the plant this time, no one bothered to complain. I sensed that so many other potential buyers had come through, no one cared anymore.

The price was right. The business wasn't. I passed again.

Facts, figures, surveys, union contracts, trends. They mean

a lot, but they still don't add up to people. If president #1 had stayed aboard, I would have made the deal. I was dazzled. Whatever "surprises" there were I would have taken in stride as part of the entry fee. And it would have worked.

But I'm equally sure I made the right decision when president #2 surfaced. The problems may have been similar, but the lack of chemistry between us almost guaranteed the kind of "surprise" subtitled "chapter 11."

MACKAY'S MORAL:

Mergers and acquisitions are like second marriages, a triumph of hope over experience. In both cases, success depends on the quality and chemistry of the people involved.

HOW I PUSHED THE ENVELOPE

SIGNED, SEALED, AND DELIVERED

Chapter 33

ONE SIZE DOES NOT FIT ALL

There used to be this picture of Nixon wearing his most dark-jowled, Nixonian expression. It was the picture that popularized the caption, "Would you buy a used car from this man?"

If the soothsayers have it right, pretty soon you won't be buying a used car from anyone. Not anyone remotely human, that is.

No more used-car lots. No sagging wires with little red, white, and blue plastic flags flapping in the breeze. No free coffee. No plaid sports coats. No salespeople. Just dial up "76–78 Pacer" on your PC and there they'll be, every mobile bubble gum machine offered for sale within a 200-mile area. Same way you'll buy your insurance, your house, your clothes, whatever. Same way you'll conduct your own business, out of the office of the future, which is no office at all.

Take the sales office version. The salesperson isn't in. Instead, he or she is in their car or in front of their PC, surrounded by the rest of the work team: a monitor, printer, modem, fax, scanner, beeper, tape recorder, cellular phone, and copier. Just master that gleaming collection of electronic tools and let's do bidness.

We've been down this road before. Every time there's a new gee whiz gizmo, we're told that we're about to embark on a replay of the Industrial Revolution.

It isn't going to happen.

The Industrial Revolution was not just about making

steam do the work of horses, it was about people moving to cities where their coworkers and companions were other people, not barnyard animals.

Computers are today's barnyard animals. They can do hard, dumb animal work a lot more quickly than we can, but they make lousy office buddies.

Salespeople may not need to go to offices to *sell* anybody, but they need to go to offices to *be* somebody. Nobody ever came back to their car after closing The Big One and played a tape of the sales manager patting them on the back. People react to, respond to, brag to, compete with, and need, other people around them.

That's what motivates them. That's what watercoolers and coffee breaks and sales meetings and sales managers are for.

That's why the world will always be safe for bad coffee and loud sports coats.

Here's a case in point.

Let's say you've decided to buy a new builder-designed home. There are two types of builders. Builder One wears $1,000 suits and has a beautiful office. There are salespeople rushing in and out. There are plans, models, sketches, and awards everywhere. The builder takes you to the site in his Lincoln. He builds 50 houses a year. If you were to dig a little, you'd find he makes about $200,000 and, like many builders, has been overextended once or twice and maybe even gone through chapter 11.

Builder Two wears jeans. He doesn't drive you to the site, because his office is at the site. It's his construction shack. There's only one other person working there, his wife. There are no models or fancy sketches, only blueprints. His vehicle is a pickup. He builds eight to 10 houses a year. If you were to dig a little, you'd find he makes about $200,000 and, like many builders, has been overextended once or twice and maybe even gone through chapter 11.

Their houses are comparably priced and constructed. They both make the same amount of money and have the same track record as businesspeople. Number one has a higher nut that he overcomes by volume, and number two makes more bucks per house by holding down the overhead.

The only significant difference is you, the customer. I would be willing to bet my last dollar that one of these two builders would be just the sort of person you would be comfortable doing business with, while the other would be a complete turnoff.

And no matter which was which, you would get about the same quality house for about the same price. That's the difference selling/marketing/image/human contact makes.

Undeniably, there are people who prefer no individual at all, but would rather deal with something as impersonal as a computer.

And that's where all the buzz is coming from lately. Well, now they've got their salesperson and we have ours.

MACKAY'S MORAL:

No computer can or ever will be able to duplicate the kind of impression one individual will have on you, another individual.

Chapter 34

RETAIL IS DETAIL

Some of the biggest breakthroughs in modern selling have been pioneered by huge national retail chains. Savvy managers and marketers are applying the same tactics in a host of other businesses, with equally impressive results. Think retail has nothing new to teach you? Think again. . . .

1. Your cash register is not just an adding machine, it's a marketing machine.

Are you using the information captured in your cash register to manage your inventory, your displays, your advertising, and your staffing?

2. Loyalty deserves to be treated like royalty.

Do you pay special attention to your best customers or do you take them for granted? Do you even know their names?

One of the reasons gambling establishments have become so successful is that they treat their best customers with a respect shown by almost no other retail establishment. As soon as Mr. Bailey establishes a minimum credit line, the dealers begin to call him "Mr. B." And the list goes on from there to include complimentary hotel rooms, free meals, a V.I.P. lounge, private gaming rooms, and a host of other perks.

What does it cost the casino to show a little extra respect? Very little compared to their earnings. What does it gain them? The most valuable asset any business can have: loyal customers.

3. Technology is not an option, it is an imperative.

Managers who pride themselves on being "computer igno-rant" are half right—they are ignorant, period. There is no excuse for not getting technologically up to speed. No matter what your responsibilities, even if you're just "thinking," you can improve your productivity and performance by learning rudimentary computer skills.

4. You can't say "whoa" when there is no finish line.

Okay, you've got a good location, so your store is "convenient."

Great, but it isn't enough.

You've expanded your hours.

Great, but it isn't enough.

You've speeded up checkout.

Great, but it isn't enough.

What's enough?

There is no enough, because there is no horizon on satisfy-ing customers' desires.

Today, assortment is the differentiator for supermarkets.

Who knows what it will be tomorrow.

Customer satisfaction is a moving target. If you don't move with it, you'll miss the mark.

5. Get with the program.

Does your store say "pantry" when the customer is saying "kitchen"?

Does your store say "kitchen" when the customer is say-ing "garden"?

You're not selling merchandise. You're providing a shop-ping environment that's compatible with the customer's lifestyle. Are you selling them what you want to sell, or are you selling them what they want to buy? If your vision doesn't square with their vision, it's adios.

6. Training is not a once-in-a-lifetime experience.

Lawyers are required to take continuing legal education in

order to maintain their licenses to practice. That kind of requirement should apply to everyone, even envelope peddlers.

Everything changes. Yesterday's training will not meet today's challenges. For your sake, for your employees' morale, for your customers' needs, keep your people up to date on products, service, and quality. You don't have to do it in a formal classroom setting; it can be delivered on an as-needed, just-in-time, shift-starting, "heads up" basis. But do it.

7. In the supermarket business, one rotten apple is one too many.

Courtesy is rule one. Grocery shopping isn't like browsing at a bookstore or buying party shoes. The customer in a business-supply store, a super-drugstore, or a huge grocery outlet is almost always in a hurry, and often regards stock-up shopping as a mindless chore. If their experience is bad because one of your people wasn't courteous, you can do everything else right and it won't matter; they won't be back.

Grocery stores can learn a thing about hospitality from the folks at Marriott. They've preached for years the axiom "make eye contact with every guest." They know that if they focus on eye contact they'll wind up with courtesy.

Customer relations training is imperative for entry-level people, who might not have learned the rudiments of courtesy. You're going to have to teach them.

8. Don't turn a temporary advantage into a permanent enemy.

Ever wonder why politicians of widely differing ideological stripes can be such good personal buddies? Because they know that today's opponent is tomorrow's ally and cosponsor.

Business types seem to have a harder time with this concept.

In recent years, much of the clout has shifted from the manufacturer to the supermarket retailer. The best retailers still cultivate strong partnerships with their suppliers. Remember, you're both trying to sell to the same customer—the consumer.

Adversarial relationships don't work over the long run. Things change. Don't burn your bridges.

9. Don't talk yourself into a deal you don't really want.

Hiring the wrong person for the job just to "maintain a relationship" or because they seem like a "nice person"? Taking stock you know your customers won't buy just to do someone a favor? Better to practice tough love. No good deed goes unpunished. In the long run, both parties will be hurt.

10. On the other hand, never say no for the other person.

Don't talk yourself *out* of a deal by assuming the other person won't be interested. Your customers won't buy ethnic foods? That's what they said about pizzas and bagels. Are you sure the supplier holds the hammer? Maybe they're overstocked. Don't automatically conclude they won't or can't lower the price, or improve the terms, or sweeten the deal to make a sale.

11. You can't drop a stone in the water without making waves.

When manufacturers talk about adding coupons, they are looking at the issue of brand loyalty. That's a key piece in the loyalty puzzle. But you need to look at loyalty from every angle. What about transaction time at the register? If the guy across the street is keeping customers waiting, that's an opportunity for you. Look for strengths and weaknesses in all your competitors and learn from them. What others do impacts you.

12. How will you know what they're thinking unless you know what they're reading?

Do you read your trade journals? That's smart. Now read your suppliers' trade journals. That's twice as smart.

13. No one says you have to do it all yourself.

You don't draft all your contracts. You hire a lawyer. You don't prepare the store's tax returns. You hire an accountant.

More and more big-volume retail managers are looking into outsourcing. Transportation is the hot area for this these days.

And how about marketing? When was the last time you sought help from a marketing guru? I guarantee you, if you're not asking for advice, you're missing an opportunity to learn.

Do what you do best. Let somebody else do the rest.

14. Do your savings cost more than they save?

Always calculate the real cost of the deal. Did you save money on shipping by taking deliveries at odd hours? If the price you negotiated results in paying overtime or shifting more work onto the backs of your own organization, you may not have saved the money you thought you did.

Often, the devil is not in the *deal*, it's in the *details*.

15. More deals result from who you know than what you know.

Your job? Your hires? Your leading advisors? Your best business opportunities? You didn't find them under a toadstool. They're the result of a lifetime of networking. Building contacts is the key to building a successful business. The best buyers and managers in the retail industry always have the freshest, most up-to-date Rolodex.

When they need to know, they really need to know.

16. If they try it they'll buy it.

Deli and gourmet sales are a powerful engine driving the modern grocery business. Providing the customer with tasting samples is fundamental to building a great deli. Sampling is much more than a product introduction. Offering food sends a strong psychological message; it is a traditional means of bonding and demonstrating friendship and hospitality. Your sample servers have an enormous opportunity to build your business. Do they have the right attitude? Have they been thoroughly trained?

17. Just because it's negotiable, doesn't mean it has to be negotiated.

Are you in a position to name your price and/or your terms? Then do it. The greatest tycoons in history were at their best figuring out what they *didn't* need to negotiate.

18. Admit your mistakes.

Any form of retailing is an art, not a science.

Listen to your customers. Survey them.

Listen to your cash register.

Listen to your employees.

Listen to your instincts.

Don't ride a loser into the ground. Cut your losses. Immediately.

Personnel. Products. Prices. Location. Marketing.

19. The first principle of pricing.

It's not how much it's worth. It's how much people are willing to pay. Too many people confuse "cheap" with "value." Good retailers understand what their customers value. Sometimes it's price. Other times it's service, comfort, access to information and/or environment. Do it right and people will pay more. Dumb down and they won't. It's up to you.

20. Beware the naked man who offers you his shirt.

(Hmmm. Why do I keep repeating this line?) New supplier with a deal too good to believe? Trying to buy your business? A questionable reputation?

Unless you've got tremendous experience and an infallible gut, let someone else try it first.

MACKAY'S MORAL:

The wise person digests the aphorism and throws the cookie away.

Chapter 35

RETAIL IS DETAIL II

1. My time is your time.

It's hard to attract part-time workers. Don't insist on a rigid work schedule because all you'll get is a lot of sick calls and no-shows. Find out when they want to work and schedule them in that time period. Flex time is big-time.

2. Don't play hide and seek.

Is your merchandise displayed where customers can find it? Resist the temptation to trap your customers in the store for hours, roaming the aisles and pawing through merchandise to find what they want. Help them save time, and you'll get more of their business.

3. What's new, pussycat?

Who says shopping has to be boring? Successful retailers know how to generate excitement even when they're selling the same stuff as everyone else. Do your displays have eye appeal? Do you change them frequently so customers want to come back to see what's new? Do you energetically promote new themes, new merchandise, new seasons, new fashions? The song goes "Life is a cabaret, old chum," not "Life is a warehouse filled with tired, old merchandise piled up in stacks."

4. Feedback means greenbacks.

They're holding an election in your shop today. The ballot box is your cash register. Are you paying attention to the results? Do you have the technology to give you constant, immediate, unfiltered feedback on what's selling and what isn't? If you don't, you better have your concession speech prepared, because your customers are voting with their pocketbooks for somebody else.

5. You have to earn your stripes every day.

Blind customer loyalty has gone the way of the Ma-and-Pa grocery. The consumer has so many choices there's no need to give an incompetent retailer a second chance. Low price? Service? Quality? Style? Whatever your niche, you'd better deliver.

6. A change for the better.

Do you always take the same route to the office? Park in the same spot? Time to try a different approach, and you'll see your store(s) in a whole new light. Do you walk your store(s) every day?

I love Ken Blanchard's philosophy that all managers should go out and walk their plants or offices and catch someone doing something right. And then in front of mother, God, and country, praise the heck out of them.

7. K.I.S.S.

You've all heard of K.I.S.S., which means, "Keep it simple, stupid."

An updated version of that story was provided by Jim Carville, who ran Bill Clinton's campaign in 1992. Every day he saw to it that his loquacious tiger got this message: "It's the economy, stupid." Clinton got the message and won the election.

8. Growing pains.

Successful generals do not outrun their supply lines. Skip the big growth opportunity if it stretches you beyond your true capabilities. Mobil is a great oil company. They proved it when they bought Montgomery Ward and nearly ran it into the ground. Businesses grow best by moving in concentric circles outward, not bold invasions far afield.

9. Tomorrow is just a day away.

It always amazes me how retailers really don't have a clue who they will be selling to tomorrow. The Census Bureau predicts Asian Americans will more than double as a percentage of the population over the next five years to more than 9 percent. What are you doing to expand your customer base among Asian Americans? Are you advertising in Asian American newspapers? Are you stocking merchandise that appeals to an Asian American clientele?

10. Who has the hammer?

This tip applies to retail just as much as it does to buying a used car. That's why I'm repeating it here.

Make sure the person you're dealing with has the authority to make a deal. Never negotiate with anyone who has to "go back and get the boss's approval." That gives the other side two bites of the apple to your one. They invariably will take any deal you are willing to make and retrade it.

11. You gotta know the territory.

Wanna buy the Brooklyn Bridge? It would be a helluva deal if the government decided to privatize the road system and let you charge tolls for it. Never underestimate the power of public policy in affecting buying decisions. The courts have yet to speak the last word on the nuances of home shopping and the sales tax, but the fact is that a huge portion of the credit card–intensive, home-shopping sales are generated because most of them exclude the sales tax.

12. Cobranding can be a grand invention.

Look for leverage opportunities that can unlock hidden

value. For example, some spectacular partnerships have emerged in cobranding credit cards with restaurants, airlines, etc. Should you be doing some of this?

13. No place like home?

Analyze the actual costs associated with offering a house credit–card system as opposed to accepting and promoting major national credit-card suppliers.

14. Keep your promises.

We are judged by what we finish, not by what we start. Initiative is important. Finishative is vital. The difficult schedule. The special order. The tough-to-fit fit.

15. Do your homework.

When a customer creates a shopping list after going through all those circulars in the Sunday paper and scanning all that background on Web sites, they have done their homework.

Have you done yours? Are you talking to customers daily? Are you talking to customers who favor the competitor's stores over your own to find out why? Information beats instincts every time.

16. Set the table to fit the meal.

You don't serve champagne in paper cups. Smart retailers don't sell merchandise. They create an environment that motivates their customers to sell themselves on an item. Is it the product's image? Is it the need to get a bargain? Is it the desire to express a certain lifestyle? You can make the sale if you know how to tell the tale.

17. It's when, not what.

You can sell anything if your timing is right. Look at the stock market. Buy low? Sell high? Great advice, but contrary to human nature. Most people buy when prices go up and sell when they go down. Smart retailers know how to ride the zeitgeist. They keep margins high when demand is great and cut their losses quickly when the tide turns.

18. If you have to make a deal, you shouldn't be dealing.
Never enter into a negotiation unless you know you can get up from the table without making a deal. The other side can always tell when you need to deal more than they do.

19. Try to draw a useful lesson from every new experience.
One of the biggest lessons of the Olympics: People want to be where the action is. Traffic? So what. Bombs? We can handle it. Stay home and watch on TV? Forget it. If you've got an attraction that attracts people, you can't keep them away.

Build it—right—and they will come, though, as Yogi Berra said, "No one goes there anymore. It's too crowded."

20. Go back and reread 1 through 19.

MACKAY'S MORAL:

Yogi Berra put it this way, "If the people don't want to come out to the park, nobody's going to stop them."

Chapter 36

THE DAY "BUYER BEWARE" BECAME "BEWARE OF BUYERS"

The difference between a strong poker player and a weak one lies in his or her ability to read the other players' cards. Strong players learn to interpret their opponents' "tells," the subtle body language that tips off their hands.

It's a rare gift, and one that is generously rewarded at poker tables and high-level negotiations. But ironically, there are lots of folks out there who have acquired the same kind of knowledge of their opponents, yet whose talents aren't being used, and when they are, they are usually underpaid and underappreciated.

They are buyers.

The only difference between buyers and those others who make their living reading people's minds is that many of the best buyers learned their trade through experience, not natural talent.

They started out as salespeople.

During my first year peddling envelopes, I got a hot lead from a friend of mine. The account used envelopes by the boxcar. They were a big mail order house in Chicago. I waltzed into the buyer's office, having practiced my best jokes in front of the bathroom mirror that morning, ready to make my pitch.

The buyer pulled out a blue envelope with two-color printing on it, and flipped it onto my lap. He said, "I want to buy five million of these from you, and here's what I'll pay per thousand." He began writing on the back of another envelope:

1. Your paper cost is	$2.80
2. You're entitled to a 5 percent markup	.14
3. Two-color printing	.46
4. The box is	.03
5. The carton is	.04
6. I'll give you 5 percent commission	.18
That adds up to	$3.65

"That's it, pal. . . . I'll give you 24 hours to think about it. . . . Give me a call . . . and say, if you've heard any good jokes lately, tell Marge, the receptionist. She just loves 'em."

I sat there in stunned silence.

Twenty-three and a half hours later I accepted the offer. I had managed to con both my estimator and myself into believing that maybe, over a long, long time, I could make up the skinning I was taking on this down and dirty price.

"Tell me," I said to the buyer when I called back, "where did those numbers come from?"

"Oh, those? Well, I used to be just like you, pal. I flogged envelopes for Central Envelope Company for 10 years before I switched to this job."

Surprise! The buyer knows more than the peddler. Of course. He used to be a peddler.

Guess who wins the negotiation.

Why has this brilliant strategy eluded so many of our corporate masterminds?

For years, I have watched big, smart companies hire buyers without a week of sales experience and give them the authority to spend tens of millions of their big, smart bankrolls on merchandise and supplies.

These days buyers get maybe $50,000 a year, plus a pretty

good dental plan. They come and they go. The sellers make six figures for starters. They know their product—and their competition—from the plant floor to the buyer's delivery dock.

Who are you betting on to win the negotiation this time?

The popular wisdom is that so many criminal defendants get off because our laws are too lenient. Maybe, but there's another reason. Many top notch criminal lawyers start out as prosecutors, and then switch to defense where they can make five times as much as we are willing to pay prosecutors. They know the problems, the pressures, the strategies of their opponents. They have sat on both sides of the table. They have superior knowledge. They tend to win.

Over a period of a lifetime, we all make big-ticket purchases. Unless we are born with the gift of being able to decipher the true meaning of a twitch of the eyebrows or a glance at the chips, knowledge, real knowledge of both side's positions is the weapon that sets the price and wins the war.

As for that supersharp buyer that gave me my MBA in one pit stop, I hired him a few years later as my executive vice president and general manager when I went into business myself. He stayed for 10 years and was the main reason why we are where we are today. . . . Thanks, Ralph.

MACKAY'S MORAL:

The best way to see around corners is to spend some time in the neighborhood.

Chapter 37

THE WISDOM OF DIRTY HARRY

I'm always amazed when I ask someone who their customers are and they say "everyone." You can't log on with that one. "Everyone" equals "no one."

I make and sell envelopes. Everyone uses envelopes. So is everyone my potential customer? No way. The margins in the envelope business are paper thin, so my profitability depends on volume, huge volume. That eliminates 99.9 percent of the world's envelope users.

Geography does it for another 99.9 percent. Delivery costs are a huge factor in bidding an envelope job. Almost any envelope company within 25 miles of a customer can offer a similar product at a better price than another outfit a couple of hundred miles away.

That's why there are few national envelope companies. We all carve out our little territories and protect them like pit bulls.

Who are my customers? They are relatively few, but they are very, very precious to me. Everyone has his or her own special needs, requirements, and quirks. Knowing what those are and how to respond to them is not just a concern. It's a career.

It's the same for every salesperson.

Your success does not depend on your product, no matter how universal or indispensable you think it is. It depends on how well you know your customers.

It means meeting their needs before they even know they have them.

The same advice applies even when you're not calling on customers, but are buried somewhere in the bowels of the corporate bureaucracy.

You're still in sales.

Your prospect is your boss.

Dave held down a customer service/expediter-type slot with a big outfit. Sound boring? Dave thought so, too. Dave realized if he ever were going to get anywhere, he'd better know more about some aspect of the business than the four other guys doing the same job. He became an expert in postal regulations. He made friends with a number of postal employees. It wasn't long before his co-workers—and his boss—came to him for help on mailing regulations. In about six months he transformed himself from just another slot-filler to a valuable resource. As the company grew, direct mail became the single largest department. Today Dave is the director of corporate services (which include mailing) and his old boss's boss. He supervises more than 200 employees.

Think about cars. The Edsel was supposed to be the greatest car ever made. The car barely had time to rust (you have to realize I'm from Minnesota) before sales ran out of gas and it became an embarrassment to Ford.

How about the minivan market? Lee Iacocca brought Chrysler back from the grave with the Dodge Caravan and Plymouth Voyager. Ford and General Motors kept their big-car mentality far too long and paid the price. Chrysler knew its customers were Baby Boomers who wanted a change from the traditional station wagon. Pull into any school parking lot now when it's time to pick up the kids and you'd swear you were at a minivan convention.

Years ago many computer companies grew by filling the niches IBM wasn't serving. IBM couldn't be bothered with niche markets. They were too big; the niches were too small. Their strategy was to wait until those markets developed sufficiently to become profitable. Then they would roll in and co-opt the customers with their own products.

It turned out that the little companies serving the little niches were on to something. Increasingly, end users wanted their own work stations, not the big mainframes IBM made. By the time IBM woke up, it was too late. The customers they had hoped they could co-opt had already found the products that met their needs.

A sadder and wiser IBM is now back in the game, but not before they got a new president, this time a marketing guy from R.J. Reynolds, and a new attitude about serving their customers.

This cautionary tale has not been lost on me. I'm aware that waiting around for a customer to meet my requirements is a lot riskier than me meeting their requirements, even when they are a little too small or a little too distant to be predictable. No, not everyone is my customer. We don't need *every* customer, just the *right* customers.

MACKAY'S MORAL:

"A man's got to know his limitations."

—Dirty Harry

Chapter 38

FOLLOW
THE LEADER

Bill Gove was a legend as a salesman at 3M. He used to tell this story in his motivational talks to the troops.

"I was just starting out in sales when my boss called me in and said, 'Bill, I want you to go to New Orleans and see our fieldman, Harry. You've never met anyone like him. He's about 60 pounds overweight, his clothes look like a bulletin board of whatever he ate for lunch, he garbles his words, and he writes his orders on the back of a napkin.'

"So I said, 'Sure, I'll go down there. What do you want me to do? Buy him a copy of *Dress for Success*? Put him on a diet? Fire him?'

" 'Hell, no. Find out what this guy is eating and make sure he gets all he wants. He's our biggest producer. And while you're down there, you'd better get some for yourself.' "

That story always worked. Maybe because it was so close to the Abe Lincoln version: "But Mr. President, Grant drinks!" "Find out what his brand is and send him a case. I need him. He fights."

Could a curmudgeon like Harry or a boozer like Grant be successful today? Of course. You see it all the time in sports. The basketball player who averages 20 points a game is on a longer leash than the backup guard. It isn't fair, it isn't right, but it's the way of the world in a world where results often matter more than how you get them.

Bill Gove and I used to tell young salespeople, "If you can

sell, don't worry about the paperwork. We'll get someone to take care of it." All kinds of people can fill out forms . . . few can really sell.

These days, with everything so techie, there's less tolerance for the klutz, even a mad demon of a salesperson klutz, because a screwup on-line can cost the company zillions. Harry's mustard-stained napkins might not pass muster, no matter how big the order.

Earl is the opposite of Harry. The word that fits him is "bearing." He walks around like he's on his way to chair a board meeting. Earl's paperwork is perfect, his desk is neat. He's on time for every sales meeting, and without having to be begged, he automatically takes a seat in the front row. Earl would be the perfect salesperson except for one thing: He couldn't give away envelopes to Publishers Clearing House. Customers just don't warm up to him.

Most salespeople fit somewhere in between Harry and Earl, not daring to be as nonconformist as Harry, but able to avoid setting people's teeth on edge, à la Earl.

Smart companies have come to realize that salespeople need to be rid of duties that have nothing to do with sales. They know that the most productive time salespeople have is the time they spend with their customers, not with their fellow employees. They—and their salespeople—are externally focused. Totally.

Dumb companies remain enmeshed in structure, processes, and politics. They tend to be internally focused on the company culture, the company rule book, the company dress code, and the company haircut. They have meetings to see if they should have meetings.

Company committees? Internal planning projects? There's Earl in the front row again, his hand raised, volunteering for the job. Earl knows his future isn't in sales; it's in getting into the bureaucracy. When the Earls of the world get promoted as their reward for doing the grunt work that successful sales-people hate, guess what happens? The regimen of regular sales meetings, new forms to fill out, and mandatory attendance take a big leap skyward.

Will Harry's production go up when Earl gets through with him? Of course not, but Harry might make less noise when he eats.

Many of you reading this may work for Earls. Don't toss in the towel. Just keep your own priorities straight. Try not to let Earl waste too much of your time, and just keep shaking and baking.

MACKAY'S MORAL:

If you're going to be different, you'd better produce. Most managers hate mavericks, but all managers love results.

Chapter 39

BIRTH OF A SALESPERSON

How can you spot a good salesperson?

I've been a salesperson for almost 40 years and I've been hiring them for just under 40 years. I think I can tell whether or not someone will make it in sales.

First, forget about age, shape, race, creed, or gender. That won't give you a clue.

Second, good salespeople make good first impressions. No one was ever sold anything by someone they didn't like. Are they genuine? Pleasant? Easy to talk with? Are they neat and well groomed? Underdressed or overdressed? Shoes are a good indicator. Not too new, but freshly shined.

Third, a powerful motivation is the engine that drives sales. Every good salesperson I've ever encountered is driven. They have a strong work ethic and a high energy level. They work longer and harder than their peers. How can you tell if they measure up here? Ask about their role models. Did they admire Mom or Dad for going out after dinner to take care of a customer? Did a teacher or a coach work tirelessly to help them learn a new skill or perfect a latent talent? High marks.

Or was it some remote historical figure? Be careful. Find out why. What was their first job? What did they learn from it? Why did they get it? How did they get it? Look for ingenuity and assertiveness, qualities to be dearly prized in salespeople.

Fourth, look for a need to be liked. Good salespeople want to please their customers. It shows. It shows in the way they go the extra mile. Calling their customers by name. Learning their customers' preferences. Keeping their customers informed. Good salespeople don't sell. They listen. Carefully. They are patient, not pushy. They know that today's sale is a lot less important than tomorrow's relationship.

Weak salespeople want to please themselves, so they push whatever is easiest to sell or carries the highest commission, regardless of the customers' needs. That shows, too.

Fifth, a service mentality. Good salespeople have second sight . . . they can see things from the customer's point of view. They willingly go beyond their traditional job descriptions to be sure that everything gets done right . . . and on time. These are the people breaking down the barriers at *boundaryless* corporations like General Electric. These are the salespeople who come out with the delivery truck to see that an installation is handled properly, who personally take care of the customer's complaint, who hound the factory until the customer's order is filled to the exact specifications.

They see their relationship to their customers differently from the way weak salespeople do. For the good salesperson, it's a long-term commitment, not a one-night stand. They insist that things be done to the customers' satisfaction. They not only want their customers to come back, they want them to tell others and make them customers, too.

Sixth, attitude. Everyone has problems—business problems, family problems, financial problems, health problems. Good salespeople leave them at home; they don't bring them to work and lay them on their coworkers and customers.

Seventh, competitiveness. Good salespeople keep score. They want to be better than anyone else and when they are, they want to be better than themselves.

Curt Carlson, the multibillionaire who founded the Carlson Companies, started out as soap salesman at Procter & Gamble. He broke every sales quota the company ever set for him. So at the start of every year, Carlson wrote down his own, considerably higher, goal. Halfway through the year, when he'd top that, he'd tear it up and write down an even bigger number to carry him through the end of the year. He's in his early eighties, he still is active in his own company, and he just keeps on writing down bigger and bigger numbers. The last time I looked, he had set a sales goal of $25 billion worldwide under the Carlson brand. Anyone want to bet he won't top it?

Eighth, a fanatical attention to detail. Good and sloppy are the oil and water of the sales game. They don't mix. Good salespeople don't sell bad products. They check to be sure defective goods don't make it out of the shop.

They keep accurate records. They know who bought what, when they bought it, and, because they are masters of their trade, they know when it's time to give the customer a call for a reorder.

Ninth, product knowledge. Weak salespeople see themselves as gatekeepers who are there to exact a fee from the customer for the privilege of buying the product. Wanna buy? Fine. Wanna ask me a complicated question about specs? Sorry, not my department. Ask an engineer.

Strong producers know their products backward and forward. They earn their commissions by providing a service: being certain the customer gets exactly what he or she wants and needs.

Tenth, self-improvement. Good salespeople are constantly working to become better salespeople. They take courses. They read books. Here's a good one: *Real Heroes of Business—& Not a CEO among Them*, by Bill Fromm and Len Schlesinger. A lot of what you just read here was extrapolated from this excellent analysis of what it takes to be a good sales (and service) worker.

MACKAY'S MORAL:

Good salespeople have three priorities: their customers, their company, and themselves. In that order.

Chapter 40

5 WAYS TO RUⁱN A GOOD SALES FORCE

We've all read countless cautionary tales about once-mighty companies that lost their way. The horror stories usually blame products that haven't kept up, dumb acquisitions, weak marketing strategies, byzantine decision-making procedures, or overloaded debt structures.

There's another major reason companies hit the skids, and I have yet to see the first word written about it: mismanaging the sales force. Well, here is that first word and a few more besides.

1. Add more salespeople.

A car dealer in a midsize city had a very prosperous dealership. He had five salespeople, and they all made really good money. The owner was getting rich, but he wanted to get rich faster. "If I can make this much money with five salespeople, I can make twice as much with 10." Good arithmetic, bad idea. With five more salespeople, the original five all started making less money. Four of them quit and went to work for the competition. We're now down to six. Of those, only two of the new hires could have sold a car to a lottery winner. We're now down to one effective and two semi-effective sales reps. Sales went through the floor. No competent salesperson would sign on because they couldn't trust the owner not to do the same thing again. The dealership never recovered and eventually went out of business.

2. Cap their earnings.

Smart companies take pride in their sales forces and believe strongly in the rainmaker concept. They know and understand there are no jobs until someone makes a sale. They establish a direct, specific, and absolute correlation between the business you bring in and the paycheck you take home. The CEOs of these companies don't get their noses out of joint if one or more of their salespeople ends up the year making more money than the boss. In fact, they're proud of it. They want it to happen. THEY ANNOUNCE IT. Dumb companies with their caste systems make sure they jigger the figures so that no salesperson ever makes more than the Big Kahuna. (We wouldn't want to have hurt feelings, would we?) The message to the sales force is crystal clear: You're second-class citizens around here.

3. Boring sales meetings.

There must be a course taught somewhere titled "Show Them Who's Boss: How Corporal Punishment Inspires Superior Performance." This line of reasoning may work for motivating marine recruits when they have to crawl across the ground under a hail of machine-gun bullets or slog through a 40-mile forced march. It does not work for experienced salespeople who are required to attend weekly three-hour sales meetings. Naturally, an appointment with a customer is no excuse for missing the fun. Like an all-night party, it usually takes two or three days to get yourself going again after one of these beauties. Good performers hate meetings, and the wimps that like them usually can't sell anything anyway. The least any sales manager could do to liven things up would be to show up dressed as Kermit the Frog every now and then. Sales meetings should not always be predictable.

4. Promoting boneheads.

Many a good peddler thinks their boss is an imbecile. Best solution? Quit or transfer. Who wants to work where they don't want their customers to meet the boss? They're afraid the customer will think, "My sales rep can't be as sharp as I thought if he's reporting to someone like this." Answer: Don't try to hide your brother-in-law in the sales manager's job. It could cost you your best salespeople.

5. Smother them in detail.

Show me a salesperson who loves paperwork and I'll show you a bookkeeper, or a salesperson in the bottom half of the class. Some companies load so much extraneous stuff on the sales force, it's a wonder they ever have time to call on customers. Here's the acid test of that last wonderful project: How many orders did it bring in?

MACKAY'S MORAL:

Most companies today have similar products.
That leaves one sure way to beat the competition—
the best sales force.

---

Chapter 41

11 QUESTIONS TO ASK YOUR PROSPECT

1. Do you have exactly two minutes to discuss a product that can save you money and boost your productivity?

As you say this, take off your watch and set it on your prospect's desk. Exactly one minute and fifty seconds into your pitch—even if it's midsentence—stop, and say, "My time is up. There's one thing I want you to know about us and that's this: We keep our word. I'd be happy to continue if you'd like. Otherwise, thank you for your time. I know you're busy. Here's my card." And get up and leave. You'll be surprised how many times you're stopped before you hit the door, and how many orders you'll eventually wind up getting.

The most important relationship you can build with a customer is trust. This will take you a long way toward gaining it.

2. Can you tell me what our competition is doing better than we are?

There are only three answers to this question that go to the merits of the product: price, quality, and delivery. If you can do better on any of these, go for it. Ask for a "sample order," a tiny slice of the business to prove you can beat the competition on its terms. If the answer is still no, then you know you haven't uncovered the real reason yet.

This is when you get, "We've been doing business with them for years." "It's the boss's brother-in-law's account." "We've never had a complaint." "I'm not the one who makes the decision on this." All of them are variations on the same theme: inertia. Go back to the office, make a written proposal, guaranteeing your terms and comparing them with the competition's, and hang in there. Eventually, you'll get a piece of that business.

3. I know something about your product already, of course, but could you tell me what you regard as its most attractive features and best selling points?

Another variation on the last question. You're looking for clues that will help you learn what it is you need to do to help your prospect enhance his own product line.

4. Is there any improvement you'd like to see in your current product?

Obviously, another thrust in the same direction as the last: How can you help your prospect do a better job? If you have something in your line that can do the trick, here's the time to trot it out. If you don't have something, maybe you should.

5. Would you let us send you a free sample if you'll use it for 30 days and let me come back and find out what you think of it?

Costly, but effective. They've been doing it for years with consumer products. If you're not doing it yet, it's time to try it.

6. Even though you're not going to give me the order today, knowing what your concerns are about our product, would it be all right if I called on you again when we are able to meet those concerns?

It's tough to say no to that one.

7. I'd be happy to recommend your product to some of my own customers. Would that be all right with you?

What could be better than having a supplier who is also an unpaid salesperson for your product? If you can deliver a customer to your prospect, even if you yourself are that customer, you're bound to increase your own odds of doing business there.

8. Can you tell me of someone who might be able to use our product?

This is the one question every insurance salesperson is trained to ask. Referrals are the heart and soul of prospecting.

9. Could I give you the names of a number of people whom you know who are using our product?

The reverse side of the last question. Instead of asking for referrals, you're giving them, except when you give them they're called references. They work because they establish credibility and reliability, the all-important trust factors in any relationship.

10. Would you tell me what I can do to be of service to you in any way whatsoever?

This is the ultimate open-ended question designed to invite your prospect to test your ability to meet whatever needs he might have. If you can get him or her to make a request, and you can deliver on that request, you've got the business.

And one more for the road . . .

11. Say, is that a picture of your family? My, what a good looking . . .

Okay, I couldn't resist. I'm still a peddler at heart.

MACKAY'S MORAL:

Good salespeople don't just supply products. They are constantly looking for ways to help their customers improve their own products.

Chapter 42

HOW TO CLOSE TOMORROW'S SALE TODAY

Melvin the Haggler was on the phone.

"I've got another hot book idea for you, Harvey."

"What is it this time, Melvin?"

"Car sellers."

"You've got to be pulling old Harv's leg. Everyone picks on car sellers. That dog won't hunt, Melvin."

"You got it all wrong, as usual. I'm not picking on them. I'm praising them. I got a call from one the other day."

"What's so wonderful about that?"

"It's the first time a car seller ever called me and asked me how I liked the car I just bought."

"You'll have to expand a little on that, Melvin. I can't quite comprehend the wonder of it all."

"I must have bought 40 cars in the course of a lifetime, and I've never bought one from the same person twice. Why should I? They sink beneath the waves as soon as they get your check. Can you imagine doing business with a stockbroker or an insurance seller and never hearing from them again? Those people know how to develop a loyal customer base. Why should car sellers be any different?"

"Every salesperson should recite the 80/20 rule in the

morning the way school kids recite the 'Pledge of Allegiance,' "
I chimed in.

"Now you're getting it. Since 80 percent of your business
comes from 20 percent of your customers, you've got to cultivate
the people who have done business with you in the past. Your
entire sales strategy as a career salesperson should be based on
expanding your share of your existing customers' business."

"Do you think one phone call is proof that's what's happening in selling cars?"

"Could be. It's sure a first for me. I bought the heap about
two weeks ago and, of course, took the usual beating on the
deal. But I do like the car. That's what I told him when he
called. Then he said, 'Melvin, I am real pleased to hear that. Tell
me, how long do you usually keep a car?' 'Four years, or so,' I
said. 'I'll tell you what I'll do,' he said. 'I'll give you a call about
then and see if I can scope out something special for you. I want
to try and make you a regular customer of mine. I'm trying to
build a career based on customer satisfaction and word-of-
mouth referrals. And, of course, if you can send me any business, and I close the deal, I'll send your favorite charity a check
for $50 in your name.' "

"Sounds like that guy has a future selling iron," I said.

"Yep," said Melvin. "He even sent me a little postcard, thanking me for my business. I never got one of those before either."

"Nice, Melvin, but hard to get real excited about."

"Wait a minute, Harvey. There are so few businesses that
do this kind of thing, I can count the number of similar experiences on one finger of one hand."

"Who?"

"Bose. The stereo people. Some of their stuff isn't even sold
in stores. They advertise in the slicks. You call them, they send
you a booklet and you order by phone. I did. I got my set the
next day, Fed Ex, and a week later, someone was on the phone
to me asking how I liked it."

"Nobody else does that?"

"No one I know of."

"But it's so simple, so easy, such an obvious way to build up a client base. Every salesperson should: *(a)* send their customers a thank you note; *(b)* call their customer within a week after the sale and ask them if they are satisfied with their purchase; *(c)* remind them that when they get around to looking for a replacement for the model they just bought, that the salesperson would be delighted to do business with them; and *(d)* there's a discount or a spiff of some kind in it for them for any referrals that result in sales."

"Harvey, a cup of water can keep you going for a day. Find a well and you can go back to it year after year after year."

"Melvin, you're a genius."

MACKAY'S MORAL:

It's not the sale that makes a salesperson. It's
what he or she does to ensure the next sale that
makes that person a pro.

Chapter 43

CRUNCH TIME

When I was a kid, one of my favorite ballplayers was Eddie Stanky. He had a lifetime batting average of .268. Hardly the stuff of legends. The dish on Stanky was, "He can't hit. He can't run. He can't field. He can't throw. He just knows how to beat you."

They called Reggie Jackson "Mr. October." He called himself "the straw that stirs the drink." Both descriptions were accurate. Jackson came alive when the World Series was on the line. He was not the most beloved guy on the team, but I never heard his managers complain when they were cashing their World Series checks.

Great players thrive under pressure. There's a moment in almost every game when it could go either way. It's called "crunch time." How you react when that moment comes is what really matters.

There's a "crunch time" in sales, too.

Any salesperson can go through the routine of a sales call without much trouble. Opening banter. Formal pitch. Questions and answers.

I was talking with a top-notch sales pro the other day, and he told me, "It doesn't take Zig Zigler to write up an order that falls into your lap. Ninety-nine percent of the time I do everything pretty much the same as everyone else and I get pretty much the same results. What I do in the other five minutes is what determines where my kids go to college."

Every sales job is different. Whatever your line, it still comes down to the same thing: the moment of truth, the part the whole sale hinges on. How you handle it separates the superstar from the bench jockey.

You can carry out a textbook sales call, but if you blow the close, you don't make the sale.

Sometimes the most important part is in the approach. You may have only a few seconds to convince your prospect that he or she would find it worthwhile to listen to you.

Many of you are dealing in price-sensitive situations and your company is never the low-cost supplier. Don't kick yourself because you think you can't sell your high-priced product. Think of what a miserable job it is to work for the company that's always the lowest-cost producer. Haggling over pennies. Cutting corners on quality. Disappointing performance. Unhappy customers.

Some of the highest paid sales pros work for the highest priced vendors. They're able to convince their prospects that it's to their advantage to pay the extra money.

"Mr./Ms. Customer, let me tell you about the team that backs up this product. We put our resources into making it and training the people behind it. That makes us a little different from the others. We pay more to get more. More quality. More research. Better reliability. Better performance. Better service. Better resale. Better people. We don't just sell it and walk away. We'll be there for you. Always. It will cost a little more now, but it's going to cost a lot less in the long run."

It's called the value-added approach.

There are salespeople who understand value so well they make it the centerpiece of their presentation.

They wait for the prospect to make the inevitable price objection and then use their response as the launching pad for their close.

They take pride in selling products that cost more than the competition. They're convinced they're providing their customers with the best value for the money. Instead of being defensive, they go on the offensive.

Did I say every sales job is different? Well, so is every sales situation. It's not always easy knowing when "crunch time" will arrive. Is it when objections are raised? Is it getting to talk to the right people? Is it the resale after a customer's so-so experience the first time around?

Many salespeople spend their entire careers learning a paint-by-the-numbers approach without really understanding the selling process. There comes a time when you have to reach beyond the obvious if you're going to connect with the prospect.

In sports, it's called hitting the sweet spot. It takes a lot of practice to do it consistently. But once you do it, you'll never be satisfied with anything else.

MACKAY'S MORAL:

A base hit looks the same in the box score whether it comes in the first inning of a "laugher" or the last inning of a one-run game. But they're not the same. It's when you make the hits that determines your value to the team.

Chapter 44

MY MONEY'S ON THE BUNNY

As kids we read Aesop's fable of the tortoise and the hare. It is a cautionary tale that shows the value of strategy over tactics.

The planner/plodder wins.

The seat-of-the-pants/live-for-the-moment type loses.

Long-range planning is a strategic exercise, and every company claims to place great value on it.

Why? We all know we're never going to carry out the plan. The future is a giant, unhittable curve ball. The conditions we assume will exist never do. Winston Churchill was once asked to describe the most valuable talent in a politician.

"It's the ability to foretell what will happen in the future, and to explain afterwards why it didn't happen."

The value of long-range planning lies in the discipline and hard thinking the exercise requires, not in the accuracy of the forecast.

Salespeople are usually exempt from planning sessions. They're not noted for their ability as strategic thinkers or for their planning skills. That's often a mistake. A smart salesperson knows as much about the customers and the product line as anyone in the company.

I'm sure they would never admit it, but I know of a large, publicly held company that would never hire an A student as a salesperson, because anyone whose grades conformed so closely to the conventional wisdom was sure to lack a quality the company values much more than rote knowledge: creativity.

My friend Wyatt was creative, which is why he was such a helluva salesman.

Wyatt was your old-time, shoeshine-and-a-smile type of marketer. He was doing his magic for a Fortune 500 telecommunications outfit back in the days when the barriers against women in sales were just beginning to lift.

Wyatt's partner was a beautiful blond 29-year-old named Shari. Wyatt's wife, Ruth, was not enamored of the fact that they often had to travel together. Wyatt did his best to assure his wife that nothing was going on, and she grudgingly put up with it.

Let Wyatt tell the rest of the story.

"It was my 20th wedding anniversary. What could be nicer than a candlelight dinner at a fine restaurant with a good bottle of wine? Unfortunately, I was on the road at the time, and enjoyed that dinner with Shari, not Ruth. We had checked into the hotel earlier in the day. On the way to the appointment with our customer, Shari mentioned to me that her room was old-fashioned and didn't have the right outlets for her hair appliances. I offered to trade rooms with her as mine had all the juice she needed, and I had yet to find an electrical gizmo that could beautify a bald head.

"Around midnight, Ruth felt a bit lonely being abandoned on the big anniversary, so she asked the hotel operator to connect her to my room. Guess who answered the phone? Let me tell you, Harvey, I'm still married to Ruth, and anyone who can talk himself out of a jam like that is a real salesperson.

"The Harvey Mackays of the world may be able to flog a few more envelopes than the rest of the pack, but I challenge them to close that one."

Like most salesmen, strategy was not Wyatt's forte. He should have made the strategic move and figured out a way to spend his anniversary with his wife. Or come up with an alternative for celebrating twenty years of wedded bliss. At the very least, he could have notified the hotel desk clerk of the change in rooms.

Instead, Wyatt gets high marks for tactical brilliance, convincing his spouse of his innocence, undoubtedly the single greatest sales job of all time.

Americans love quick thinkers. The most exciting play in football isn't anything you'll ever find in a playbook. It's when a quarterback improvises and makes something happen when a play has broken down.

A well-known preacher was about to deliver a closely reasoned, carefully researched commentary on a complex passage in the Bible when he realized he'd left his manuscript back in the office. So he winged it. Instead of trying to impress the congregation with his scholarly erudition, he talked about what he knew best, himself, his own life, what had brought him to the ministry and how he came to be standing before them at that very moment. It was the greatest sermon he ever gave.

History is filled with examples of how a seat-of-the-pants tactic turned the tide just when things appeared to be most dire.

The near disaster of the Apollo 13 mission is that kind of story. The world's best scientists had planned the mission. Nothing could go wrong. When it did and their contingency planning didn't cover, it wasn't quantum physics, it was chewing gum, baling wire, guts, and ingenuity that saved the day.

The Betamax people thought technical superiority would let them dominate the videotape market. The VHS people won the battle because they fought it on their own turf. They ignored Betamax's strengths and concentrated on their own: marketing and distribution.

Guy Kawasaki, Macintosh's product manager, was quoted in *Twin Cities Business Monthly* as describing how Macintosh's business strategy evolved: "Lead, take a shot, listen, respond, lead again."

Sure, it's trial and error, but trial and error wins more often than no trial for fear of making an error.

MACKAY'S MORAL:

Making each day count is a tactic. Making each year count is a strategy. You need both to succeed.

Chapter 45

DON'T "CALL ME ISHMAEL," CALL ME ENVELOPE SALESMAN

I can understand why most people would be a tad reluctant to pass out business cards that identify themselves professionally as "Funeral Director," or "Proctologist," or "Gestapo Agent." But what is it about selling for a living that makes salespeople so antsy about being called salespeople? Is it because we're so used to seeing civilians cringe every time they hear the word "salesperson," afraid Willy Loman will jump out, sporting a cheap suit, a bad haircut, and sweaty palms?

Willy is gone and he ain't ever coming back, but we can't seem to shake the Loman image. Corporate America has PRed itself into developing more euphemisms for salesperson than Bill Clinton has for relationships. I'm on a one-man crusade against it. When I run across the boss of a new outfit, I ask one sneaky little question, "How many salespeople do you have on your payroll?"

They never have any. None whatsoever. And they are offended by the question.

"We don't have any salespeople around here. We have sales consultants/sales associates/sales executives/order takers/ brokers/account executives/financial planners/registered representatives/marketing engineers/product managers/regional-district-area customer-client service consultants/agents. But salespeople? No. How crude. How crass. How unlike us to admit we actually go around selling the stuff we make."

Who are we fooling here, folks?

In 1954 I got my first real job. I became an envelope salesman. It said so right on the card: "Harvey Mackay/Envelope Salesman," and I was proud as hell of it. I papered the Twin Cities from one end to the other with that baby. I laid it on every hand I shook.

It didn't take a graduate degree in macroeconomics for this envelope salesman to figure out that every time I wrote up an order, I was making the wheels go round. Sales made things happen, turned on the lights in the front office, made the machines in the plant hum. No sales, no business. Products, strategies, organization charts, may all come and go. But as long as a business stays in business, there will be a place at the table for the salesperson.

Among the numbers the Federal Bureau of Labor Statistics grinds out are these: 30 percent of all Americans hate their jobs. They are frightened of losing them, of being replaced by technological changes. They feel dead-ended. They believe they have no chance for improving their incomes, for raising their standards of living.

This unhappy statistic does not apply to salespeople. I can guarantee you that the nation's 14 million salespeople make up only a tiny fraction of the sad and the disheartened.

Because with all the mergers, acquisitions, downsizings, consolidations, restructurings, and right sizings, the sales organizations of American businesses have taken the fewest casualties. They go marching on to war.

If you are blessed with sales skills or have made your decision to enter the selling field and get some training, you have made a very wise and sound decision for your future. You can take your talent with you wherever you go. You will always be in demand. You will have unlimited income potential.

It's a good thing all of us didn't take Mom's advice. Remember how she constantly begged us to get that law degree so we would always have a profession that could support us, in good times or bad? Well, thanks a lot, Mom, but things aren't like that anymore. A few years ago, once you had a law partnership you had a better tenure deal than a mail carrier. Today, if you're not a rainmaker bringing in big billings to the firm, even a Harvard law degree and law review credentials won't save your partnership and your job. Now lawyers, accountants, architects, dentists, hospitals, medical plans, all sell, sell, sell. It took dog-eat-dog and rat-eat-rat competition to wake them up to the reality that nothing sells itself.

Including envelopes. But there is one difference in the envelope business. The difference is that 40 years after beginning my selling career, my business card still reads, "Harvey Mackay/Envelope Salesman." If it hadn't, if I had stopped selling, if I had stopped continually building and rebuilding a sales force, there would not be a second line on that card today, the line that reads "Mackay Envelope Corporation."

MACKAY'S MORAL:

Sales are the engine that pulls the train.
Everything else follows.

Chapter 46

BEWARE THE WELL-CLOTHED MAN WHO OFFERS TO BUY YOUR ENVELOPES

When I got started in the envelope business, it was a struggle to make a sale, any sale. No one had ever heard of me or my company. Even when I managed to get a foot in the door, I usually found myself being used as a stalking horse to force an established competitor to lower their price, rather than as a legitimate bidder. One day, cold calling, I decided to take a run at one of our town's major mail order houses. After all, what could they do but say no to me? Amazingly, they didn't. It was "Where do I sign?" before I even had a chance to finish my pitch.

That should have given me a clue. But no, I figured it must have been my natural charm.

Three days later, working around the clock, my ancient machinery shooting flames and billowing smoke, Mackay Envelope proudly delivered 250,000 two-color, printed #10 envelopes to my new customer. The day after that, they declared bankruptcy.

Mackay's Big Boo Boo #1: A big name on the door doesn't mean diddly. Never do business with someone unless you know that they will do what they say they are going to do. Check it out. Talk to their bank. Talk to their other suppliers (noncompetitors, of course). Talk to their competitors. Talk to their customers. A huge out-of-the-ordinary order from an unlikely source is not always a sign that the gods of commerce have smiled upon you. Quite the opposite.

My next move, after being stiffed, was to go to a very large, very prestigious, very expensive downtown law firm, where I was ushered into an office that could have been Donald Trump's. Here was the Man. My father had arranged the introduction. What an honor. What a charmer. What a disaster.

He told me a few marvelous anecdotes from his vast and storied legal career. I was duly impressed. He told me several more anecdotes. I told him my problem. He responded with still more tales of his august antics.

Just as he finished a buzzer sounded and his secretary came in and reminded him of the important meeting he had to attend. He had time for just one more anecdote as he rose and led me to the door.

Then, for three weeks, nothing.

By this time, I was tottering on bankruptcy. I needed action. Every time I called, Mr. Hotshot Attorney was in conference.

Finally, one of his underlings called me back. He asked me to repeat the whole story, which I did, and after another three weeks, Mr. Junior Clerk entered my claim. It was another six months before I got paid, a big thirty cents on the dollar.

Mackay's Big Boo Boo #1—the Reprise: Mackay, how many times does it take before you learn that a big name on the door doesn't mean diddly?

To the big rainmaker, my problem was the equivalent of a box of envelopes in terms of its economic value to him and his firm, so he shuffled it off to one of his low-paid drones. And he took his time about it, just to teach me not to bother him again with penny-ante stuff, like my survival. Thus, Big Boo Boo #1—the Corollary: Before you do business with someone, be sure you know the difference between the name on the door and the person actually doing the work. Make sure you know who he or she is. Make sure he or she knows who you are. That's why I keep getting thrown out of garages. I insist on going back into the grease pit to say hello to the mechanic. I want him to know there's a face attached to that faulty fuel pump, a face that wants the job done right.

I think I finally got it.

MACKAY'S MORAL:

Like I've always said, I try never to make the same mistake three times.

Chapter 47

LET'S DO LUNCH

One of the fine old traditions in selling is the client lunch—with a kicker: the salesperson's CEO comes along as an added attraction.

This ritual has become so institutionalized that many CEOs and managers, who have a quota of customers to meet, satisfy that quota by doing client lunches with their salespeople.

The script often goes something like this.

The boss tells the client how much they value their business, what wonderful things the salesperson has to say about him or her and what marvelous good fortune to be served by such a crackerjack salesperson. And the closer is, of course: What can we do to make our relationship even stronger?

While clients have been known to place important orders at such moments, this is also a moment for candor. An airing of problems is not uncommon, but if the stage has been set correctly, the client usually is pretty benign by this point.

When it's handled right, it's a win-win situation for everyone. The client feels valued and sees his or her concerns are being taken seriously. The salesperson gains credibility with the customer and bragging rights among his or her peers. The CEO shows both the salesperson and the customer that the boss cares and also picks up on what's going on out in the real world.

So much for the ideal.

Now for the reality.

A million things can go wrong with this scenario. Here are a few of them. CEOs and managers take note.

- **The "We'll Take Care of That" trap.**

Bosses tend to get carried away by their own eloquence. They'll promise anything. When these visionary flights of fancy strike them in their own offices, they usually don't make it out the front door. But remember, we're in the real world now, and when a customer hears it from the top, they expect it to happen.

Guess who has the job of making dreams come true? I have heard salespeople tell me of luncheons where what the CEO promised was illegal, impossible, or hadn't even been invented yet. Bosses, don't leave messes behind for others to clean up.

Your job is to back *them* up. Who's out there in the trenches every day with the customer? The salesperson or you?

- **The "Call Me If You Need Anything" syndrome.**

The point of these luncheons is to build up the salesperson, not to demonstrate how almighty and important the boss is. Too many bosses have chapped lips from kissing the mirror so often. Need anything? Call the salesperson, not me. The salesperson has the power and the company's total confidence. This person can get anything done that needs to get done. What a winner!

- **The "I'll Pick Up the Check" fallacy.**

Don't. The salesperson picks up the check. The salesperson is the big shot at the table, not the boss. The boss is a guest, just like the client.

- **The "Keep 'Em Waiting" gambit.**

Double don't. Arrive on time. You don't have to prove how important you are by having the customer and salesperson awaiting your grand entrance.

- **The "Paging the Boss" game.**

Triple don't. Accepting a page during lunch doesn't prove you're important; it proves you're rude.

How a boss handles one of these luncheons says a lot about his or her abilities as a leader.

MACKAY'S MORAL:

"Leaders think about empowerment, not control. The best definition of empowerment is you don't steal responsibility from people."

—Warren Bennis

Chapter 48

THE BLACKBOARD JUNGLE

Before Pat Harrington became a professional comedian, he was a time salesman for NBC television, then a subsidiary of RCA. Grant Tinker, in *Tinker in Television*, describes what happened at one memorable sales meeting.

One day a short, balding man strode into the room just as Harrington's meeting with his sales force was about to get started.

"I am General David Sarnoff," he announced in a thick Russian accent, taking a seat at the head of the table, "and as president of RCA, it is my custom to become familiar with every aspect of our business. Please, go on with your meeting. I'll try to be as unobtrusive as possible."

For 15 minutes, the sales force uncomfortably tried to conduct business as usual under the watchful eye of the general. Finally, he spoke. "Gentlemen, there is something I don't understand. We have rate cards here. Why is it that you never seem to make a deal where the rate conforms to the rate on your cards?"

There was a long, awkward silence. Exasperated, Harrington finally jumped in. "General, we're much too busy to play question and answer games. Why don't you haul your ass back up to the 50th floor and mind your own business?"

As the general stalked out of the room, Harrington nonchalantly resumed the meeting, ignoring everyone's gasps. It wasn't until months later that Harrington revealed he had hired an actor to play General Sarnoff.

You don't have to go that far to breathe life into your sales meetings, but if you're responsible for managing a sales force, a little planning can do more than fight off boredom, it can prevent disaster.

For example, the standard brainstorm for lagging sales morale is sales training. If your sales team comes back all charged up, it's great. But ask any veteran salesperson from one of the Fortune 500 companies, and you'll get too many war stories about training that's a waste of time. Not only is it expensive—$500 to $1,000 a pop these days—but it can keep your top guns away from their customers, and at the mercy of your competitors, for as long as a week, taking part in exercises that won't translate into one more order.

I know of a class that held 20 highly paid salespeople hostage while they spent an entire day hearing about opening new accounts. Normally that's a good subject, but these 20 people were major-account types, and each worked on a single account. They weren't selling a low-buck or one-shot product. They were deeply immersed in day-in, day-out servicing of one demanding customer. Wrong message.

I know of another large company that sent all its personnel who sold to government and education accounts to a class where a hotshot former bureaucrat spent three to four days going over government budgets and financials. The idea was that if they were familiar with them they would be able to spot areas where there was money to fund the company's target projects. It sounded good on paper, but not a single one of the 65 account executives ever used it.

A better idea would have been to teach that crew how to be positioned with the government official who had the knowledge to discuss the budget, and the clout to sign the purchase order. The pros know that if that wondrous soul can be persuaded, he or she will find the funds no matter what the budget says. They had used wrong strategy.

On the other hand, I know some fairly successful salespeople who work for small firms and have had absolutely no sales training. Sure, they've been given technical-type training. But there still are companies that believe selling isn't a profession, so why should salespeople receive professional training?

The answer is, because your sales force is going to be trained no matter what the company does; however, it's up to the company whether that training is going to be good or bad, haphazard or systematic. If everything a salesperson learns over a 30-year career is self-taught, you can bet some of it is dead wrong, and all of it will cost the company a lot more in the way of time and money than it would if the company had provided proper training.

I wonder what the real Sarnoff would have thought of the ad rates for the last episode of *Seinfeld*.

MACKAY'S MORAL:

Take the routine out of your routine sales meetings and make sure your sales training matches your salespeople's needs.

Chapter 49

HE WHO DOES THE PAYIN' DOES THE SAYIN'

In my sandbox, we don't just haggle over pennies, we haggle over one-fourth of a penny. Granted, we're talking about lots of 10,000, but it does lead to a certain healthy discipline among envelope floggers. If you expect to get the business, you better know your customer, your product, and your competition before you step onto the playground.

Years ago I heard about a start-up in my territory. They were in direct mail, an industry with an enormous appetite for envelopes, and they were going gangbusters. New account? Hot company?

I'd been in the game long enough to know that if my business was going to grow, it wasn't going to be by milking my existing accounts. When you're on a ladder, you don't go sideways. It's up or down.

So I went cold calling, but I had no intention of getting frostbite. First, I did my homework:

1. I called my friendly banker and put out a serious warrant for all pertinent information. They aren't supposed to tell you, but they do . . . as long as it's another banker's customer and not theirs.
2. I did a search at the library for any relevant newspaper articles.
3. I asked my sales force for the buzz on the buyer.

4. I asked our suppliers who supply us paper, boxes, cartons, and ink.

Now I was ready.

Fast forward to two years later.

I got the account. We were in on the ground floor. Their volume soared. So did ours.

The account became a top 10 number, and we were the sole supplier. Even when we did drop the ball—a late delivery and one smudged printing which we reran—we didn't lose any ground. My strategy was simple. I stuck to the buyer like peanut butter sticks to jelly. Lunches. Factory tours. Golf. Ball games. Economic forecasts. Industry analysis. Consumer trends. I got to where I knew almost as much about direct mail as I did about envelopes.

Competitors shied away because they knew how "close" I was to the buyer. It was perceived as Harvey's locked-up account.

Yes, it was *my* account. Mine, all mine. Forever and ever.

Until one day when I stopped by my lifetime account and the receptionist cheerily informed me, "Oh, by the way, Mr. Mackay, Tom is no longer with us. He's moving to Oregon to become a senior buyer at a Fortune 500 company. Everyone loved Tom. It took us all by surprise." Surprise? I'll say.

"Our new buyer is Greg from accounting. Do you know him?"

"Can't say that I do."

How dumb, naive, and wrong could I be?

A brand new buyer, and I didn't know Greg from Snoop Doggy Dog.

Every negative thought raced through my mind:

1. I have to start all over again,
2. Every job will now be sent out for three bids,
3. The vultures will swoop down and lowball this account just to get a beak in the door.

And guess what? All my fears came true. How I'd love to have those years of calling on that business back and make sure I knew every potential new buyer in case Tom was gone. You always want to call as high up on the ladder as possible. Also, I should have asked him for his help just in case he decided to leave.

Naturally, the new buyer wanted to spread the business around, and I got nicked pretty badly. And I deserved to be for having been lazy and arrogant. In my eyes, this was *my* account.

But it wasn't. Not ever. It was always the customer's account, and my customer was the company, not the buyer.

Since that bitter experience, things have changed here at Mackay Envelope.

We look on new business in a new way. If the current buyer has left and our salespeople have to begin again with a new buyer, we treat that account as new business. We start from scratch. We prepare a new strategy, and if we are successful, we reward our salespeople just as if they had landed new business.

MACKAY'S MORAL:

"Just because the river is quiet, does not mean the crocodiles have left."
—Dan Fuss of Lomis Sayles
(quoting an old Malaysian saying)

THE FLAP ON MANAGEMENT

FROM THE
MAIL ROOM UP

Chapter 50

A Pat on the Back Accomplishes More Than a Slap in the Face

"I love my job."

"I love my company."

"I love my family."

That's great. Just remember, the first two *(a)* can't love you back, and *(b)* are a lot easier to replace than the last one.

I attended a funeral recently and the minister read a letter that the son mailed to his father shortly before the father's death.

Dear Dad:

Mom called the other day and told me you weren't doing too well. I sure wish I could be there for you. You were always there for me. I like my job here on the coast, but I sure miss the folks back home.

I was watching television the other day and some-one talked about telling your loved ones you love them. Most of the time, I tune that stuff out, but I have to admit that for once it hit home.

Dad, I probably never told you that I loved you. Oh,

maybe I did when I was a little kid, but as I got older, I sensed that wasn't the "manly" thing to do.

We didn't hug much either. Too touchy-feely. A firm handshake was the proper way to share our feelings.

Dad, I wish I had done it differently. It's just that during my time of growing up, things were not like they are today. In those days, we took our cues from the movie tough guys. The slightest hint of affection or warmth was a sign of weakness.

I want to thank you for all you did for me. You took me to my first ball game, and when I started to play ball myself, you went to every game you could. You got me through the rough spots when I made a bad throw or struck out at a crucial moment. Learning to pick myself up and get squared away again sure helped when I was getting started in the sales game.

When I left home for the first time, I was lonely. You convinced me that it would pass and that I shouldn't be a quitter. That was another valuable lesson.

I also recall the time you caught me smoking just after I told you I wasn't doing it. It was not a pleasant encounter. You were madder than hell at me and you made me aware of your feelings in no uncertain terms, but as you know, Dad, I haven't smoked since.

I remember when I got my first real job. You gave me a pep talk about giving something extra and not being a clock watcher. When I made my first big sale, and I called to tell you, I got you out of a meeting. I was so proud. And so were you.

You always set an example for me as a husband and a father. You're not only my mentor, you're my best friend.

Dad, I love you. Linda loves you and your grand-children love you, too. Our prayers are with you.

Love,
Steve

We were all choked up by Steve's letter. The sad part about it is that it arrived the day after his dad slipped into a coma. He never got to hear it.

"I love you" isn't the only tough thing to say. There are some phrases that aren't exactly bandied around the workplace or at home that belong in everyone's vocabulary, like "You did a terrific job," "I'm sorry," "I was wrong," "I forgive you," "I believe you," "I appreciate all that you're doing," "You make me proud."

No matter if you were brought up in a marine boot camp or a royal palace, it doesn't hurt to try and slip a few of these expressions into your speech pattern. They may be a lot less common than the "F word" these days, but those you love will always remember you used them.

MACKAY'S MORAL:

Don't wait for the funeral before you pay a compliment. You may not make it in time.

Chapter 51

How Not to
Pick a Winner

Q: What is a manager's single most important task?

A: To hire people who know how to do a better job at what they do than what the manager could do, and then get out of the way so they can do it.

It sounds easy enough, but time and again managers confuse the trappings of success and the godlike power at their fingertips with expertise in areas they know nothing about.

Managers figure they're getting paid to make decisions, so they make them. But that isn't what they're getting paid for. They're getting paid to be right. And sometimes that involves knowing when not to make a decision.

Roger Smith, a financial expert who climbed the greasy pole to head General Motors, was dazzled by technology. So he bought a bazillion dollars worth of robots to make cars for GM. Robots don't strike, they don't play hooky during deer-hunting season, and they don't make movies like *Roger & Me*, which was a biting satire slamming General Motors, done by an ex-GM employee. Unfortunately, robots don't perform very well either, and even if they did, they wouldn't have solved GM's core problems of inferior design and quality control.

Harvey Mackay scored a modest success in the selling and marketing of envelopes. So I went out and blew a million bucks on a state-of-the-art envelope-making machine. Did I listen to our factory experts? Why should I? Even though I was last in my kindergarten class to master the art of tying a shoelace and have been known to call an electrician out to my house to change a light bulb, I figured if my name was on the door of the envelope company, I was the one who knew best how to make envelopes.

Move over, Roger. Anyone out there care to buy one very large envelope-manufacturing machine, in almost mint condition?

Over the years I've learned that lawyers and accountants make *(a)* terrific lawyers and accountants, and *(b)* lousy business people, but I've had a lifetime problem trying to apply the same logic to my own skills. Years ago I hired a hotshot sales manager away from one of my chief competitors. Like every salesperson, I'm a sucker for a first-rate pitch and this one was a snow job of blizzard proportions. He just walked in the door and bowled me over. He had all the credentials, on the surface—exceptional intelligence, a career envelope man, a very hard worker, creative, visionary, and he'd bring a ton of business with him. I was so positive I had struck it rich, I broke one of my own cardinal rules and didn't bother to run him by my industrial psychologist, whom I had always, until that moment, used for every key hire.

Why bother? Couldn't I tell a born sales manager when I saw one?

It turns out I couldn't.

Yes, he could sell all right, but he couldn't manage, and the slot was *sales manager*, not salesperson. Within a week, a line had formed outside my door. Each person had a horror story. Each had the same punch line: "Either he goes or I go." Just to give you one example: Our top salesperson in any given month gets the parking spot nearest the door. It doesn't sound like much, but we make a big deal out of it. There's a sign at the head of the space. At the top of the sign it reads, RESERVED FOR and under that there's a slot for inserting the name of the honoree and under that the words SALESPERSON OF THE MONTH.

As a peddler myself, I know that nothing happens at our shop, nothing moves out the door, unless a salesperson makes it happen. Salespeople usually don't get a lot of recognition at most companies, but they do at Mackay Envelope.

My new sales manager had other ideas. He had the sign removed and replaced with "Sales Manager," with his name above it.

But hey, he was my hire, so I toughed it out. I was as arrogant as he was, unwilling to admit to myself I'd made a mistake.

Not one mistake. Almost two mistakes.

Thinking my snap instincts were better than the industrial psychologist's careful, time-proven analysis. Thinking I could ignore the obvious evidence of my blunder without paying for it in blood.

After two of my best people threatened to walk, I threw in the towel.

I found a new sales manager.

And every month we have a new SALESPERSON OF THE MONTH.

MACKAY'S MORAL:

The most valuable ability is the ability to
recognize ability.

Chapter 52

HIRING A HEART ATTACK

If you managed a baseball team, would you like to have an out-field made up of *(a)* Ted Williams, *(b)* Ty Cobb, and *(c)* Babe Ruth? Of course you would. They were three of the most gifted players ever to grace the game. They are also three of the biggest head cases ever to *(1)* throw a tantrum and break a watercooler with a bat, *(2)* go into the stands to beat up hecklers, *(3)* miss practice and show up drunk at the ballpark.

Talent and emotional stability do not necessarily go hand in hand. But if you're a manager, whether it's baseballs, ball bearings, or ball-and-socket joints, the time will come when you have to decide whether it's worth the effort to hire some-one who has the job skills you need but whom you dislike personally.

How do you make the call?

First you have to ask yourself: Is it me or is it the candidate?

Be honest with yourself. Are you basing your opinion on your gut feelings or do you have real evidence that the candi-date is too hot to handle?

Here's how to make an objective call.

1. Make sure the candidate is screened both by others at the company and by an industrial psychologist. Alert the IP to your concerns before they interview the candidate. That way he or she will be able to make a more thorough evaluation.

2. Check those references closely. Do it by phone or, if possible, in person—you're much more likely to get a candid answer—and lay your specific concerns on the line.
3. Give yourself a cooling-off period and then conduct a second interview. Maybe you were having an off day. Now go back over the problem area. Ask the candidate directly.

"I'm concerned that you may have something of an attitude when it comes to taking direction. Is that a problem for you?"

"You've made several remarks about people different from yourself that bother me. Do you want to explain why you said such and such."

"When I check your references I'll want to know more about your ability to get along with others. Can you tell me about that?"

You may get an answer that explains it all, though I've been asking questions like this for 40 years and I haven't heard one yet. But, hey, it could happen.

Okay, let's say you've taken the steps described above and everything indicates the candidate is, gulp, a jerk. Well, so was Ty Cobb, but he hit .367 lifetime. You've still got to decide whether to hire or not.

What factors could make you decide in the candidate's favor?

1. The candidate has to be, far and away, the best person for the job. No one gives Barbra Streisand a Stanford-Binet test before she sings a concert; the only test they care about is at the box office. If your candidate can deliver what no one else can, read no further, the choice is obvious: you hire.
2. The double-whammy factor. Not only is the candidate an outstanding talent, but you're hiring the person away

from a competitor, so you're not only helping yourself, you're giving the competition fits.

3. Diversity, conflict, and contention may not be pleasant, but they can produce results. Every organization needs new ideas and fresh thinking. Are you getting it from the look-alike think-alikes that line your office walls? If not, it's time to get a wake up–shake up personality on board. If an anti–status quo attitude is what troubles you about the candidate, go back to square one: hire. The problem is you.

4. If you do decide to hire, make sure the candidate understands that there is a probationary period, and make it as long as possible. There's nothing the matter with giving yourself as much protection as you can in a difficult situation. And have an agreement if things don't work out either way. The best exit strategy is to part company as friends and not get into the particulars of what went wrong. No incriminations needed.

Whenever there's a major corporate merger these days—and they're taking place at a record pace—the tribal ritual is for the CEOs of the two marriage partners to stage a joint press conference. I love the photos of last month's "enemies to the death" practically jumping into each other's laps.

When Federated Department Stores and Bloomingdale's merged a few years ago, *Business Week* quoted an unnamed source as saying that one of the presidents of the two outfits said to the other, "Look, we don't have to love each other, but you're the better guy for this job."

Well, that's the test, isn't it? If these two guys can do it, so can we.

MACKAY'S MORAL:

It's not always what's up front that counts.
It's what's inside.

Chapter 53

PICK YOUR BATTLES WISELY

An engineering phrase has become a buzzword in offices around the country. Maybe some engineer got angry at a subordinate for continued tardiness and yelled, "I have zero tolerance for your continued late arrivals!" A human resources manager heard it and a star was born.

While we don't have zero tolerance on the floor of our manufacturing plant when it comes to making envelopes, it comes darn close. We knock out 15 million envelopes a day, so we have to know what we're doing. But we do have a little leeway. Our customers will tolerate one-sixteenth-of-an-inch play on the window or envelope fold. If you're one-eighth of an inch shy, "ears" can develop in the corners of the envelope making it difficult for our customers to insert material. If you're one-eighth of an inch too big, the envelope develops "holes" in the corners and looks sloppy. Bingo . . . unhappy customer.

Come to think of it, I've had zero tolerance on certain issues all my life. Like when my kids wanted a VW beetle for their get-around car in high school. I preferred the iron of a big-fendered tank. I won. Reason? Their safety.

Or the time they wanted to water-ski without life jackets, or they couldn't find the seat belt, or they wanted to go to Mexico on their spring break in high school, or they wanted to hitch-hike across the country, or they wanted to talk on the phone all night on a school night. I was the bad guy. I wouldn't give in, and I bit my lip until it bled.

However, I might have been softer than most parents on other issues. They could have as many friends sleep over at *our house* as they wanted. They could stay up all night on the weekends as long as they didn't leave the house. They could get mad at me and use a strong voice to assert their opinions. They could side with the radical left all they wanted. But they had better not ride on any motorcycles while they're on my watch.

We have, of course, had zero tolerance for some of the *wrong* things over the history of Mackay Envelope Corporation. We once had an accountant who kept track of pads of paper issued per employee, personal calls made on company time, and work breaks. No personal copying at the copy machine. Zero tolerance for zero things makes zero sense.

At Mackay Envelope we have zero tolerance for the biggies: intimidation, sexual harassment, discrimination. Zero tolerance may dictate that the dog only gets one bite if the bite is bad enough. We also don't tolerate a less-than-spectacular receptionist, endless voice mail circles, unanswered phones, verbal abuse, or people who don't like salespeople or customers.

We *do* tolerate active conversation that isn't job specific. Sometimes the watercooler looks like the highway department. We tolerate daily birthday parties and food and candy at our desks. We tolerate messy work spaces, and children and babies who are in our office for an hour or, in a pinch, a few hours. We tolerate end runs around supervisors when employees feel shunned. We tolerate dreamers and blank stares out the window—the best thinking is often done behind a blank stare. We tolerate and accept departure—not high turnover, but departure. People move on. There are 78,000 active businesses in Minneapolis and St. Paul, and we don't have a career path for every employee.

So are we running Mackay Country Club? No. We work very, very hard and, I like to think, very smart, with the customer as king, salespeople as our lead dogs in the pack, and maximum tolerance for human behavior.

> ### MACKAY'S MORAL:
>
> Reserve zero tolerance for the biggies.

Chapter 54

FISH STINK FROM THE HEAD, AND 9 OTHER SUBTLE TIPS ON MANAGING

1. Fish stink from the head.

Thank you, Al Greenberg, author of *Memos from the Chairman*. Your attitude and behavior affect every employee in the shop, top to bottom. Do you scream at your secretary? Do you duck out early? Even if your office is on the 50th floor, word will reach the guys in the boiler room quicker than you can get down the elevator and out the door.

Employee morale usually goes the way the corners of your mouth turn.

2. Do it yourself.

People are willing to take on all kinds of menial chores uncomplainingly if they're asked to do them in a courteous and reasonable fashion, and they see some benefit to themselves.

When pump jockeys began to disappear from gas stations, the service station industry reinvented itself as the no-service service station. Pump your own and save. We all do it.

Where would the fast-food industry be today if it hadn't learned to ask its customers to bus their own trays?

If you're a low-cost operation on tight margins, don't be afraid to ask your customers to help. You'll likely get just as good results as having minimum-wage workers do the job. If they show up.

3. Catch the wave, and you'll sell the suds.

Several years ago, the trend in the brewery biz was micro-brewers. So what did the biggies do? Reinvented themselves as tiny operations from obscure hamlets in the backwoods of Wisconsin.

Fast forward a couple of years: it's macrobrews again. Who knows what next year will bring? The one thing you can be sure of is that all beer tastes pretty much alike. It's the marketing that sells it.

Remember the Cutlass Supreme or Achieva? Seen any ads lately? Not likely. The cars were phased out. But there's plenty of action for Alero, a product that barely acknowledges its Olds heritage.

What are you doing to define your product or service in line with today's trends? Does your menu look like an artifact from the Eisenhower years? Is your packaging up to date? Is your advertising reaching your target audience?

Your product or service may be great but you can't sell it by shouting into a rainbarrel. Smart outfits, huge outfits, aren't too proud to change their themes or even their names, if it means selling their goods.

Kentucky Fried Chicken became KFC right around the time "fried" became a dirty word. The product, and its profits, are still finger lickin' good.

4. No deal is better than the people you are dealing with.

No contract can save you from an out-and-out crook. Even if you know you have an ironclad lawsuit or a claim against the other party if they default, it's far better to deal with an honest person to begin with, and save yourself the lawyer's fees—and the aggravation.

You lie down with dogs, you get up with fleas.

The second most important item in any contract is having one, in writing.

5. Never make a major decision off the top of your head or from the bottom of your heart.

There is no more certain recipe for disaster than an instant decision or one based on emotion. Sleep on it. Take your time. Consider all the angles. Be patient. Even if you're trading pork bellies, you are paid to be right, not paid to be quick. Don't go off half-cocked. Get all the information, get all the advice. Then act. Decisively. No one ever remembers how long it took to reach a decision, only what the result was.

6. Who's listening?

Everyone has training sessions these days. No one seems to have a clue as to whether the trainees have learned anything or not.

Why not find out?

At the end of the day, hold an unannounced pop quiz. You will be surprised—and disappointed—at the results. For one thing, you'll discover that some of your supposed participants will have ducked out after lunch.

That's the first time.

The second time you do it, word will have gotten out.

Two things will happen.

One, attendance at the training session will go down.

Why? Because duck-outers will not sign up.

Two, the test scores will go up.

7. How to win at liar's poker.

We all lie. Out of fear. Out of politeness. The motives are endless. When a prospect says no, and bases it on price, money is almost never the real reason. Usually, the prospect has been a long-time customer of another supplier. A combination of inertia, fear of change, fear of upsetting a pleasant relationship, fear of being criticized if the new supplier doesn't work out, all combine to generate that "no."

How do you overcome it?

Smart salespeople know that you can't confront the prospect directly. You accept the situation as it is. You have to make time and familiarity work to your advantage.

You try to position yourself not as the new "number one," but as "number two."

Okay, so the prospect has cast the star role and it isn't you. All you want is to be the understudy, to learn the part so that you can step in and fill the breach if the star should ever stumble.

And stumble they do. They retire. They change jobs. They mess up.

Anything can happen.

And when it does, hey, a star is born.

8. And the last shall be first.

Have they cast the star role in your industry? That's all right. Second place is the best place from which to launch changes, to modernize, to upgrade, to experiment, to try new products, to offer new services.

When you're in second, you don't have to be frozen with fear that any change you make will jeopardize your standing. You can make moves that the folks in first are afraid to try.

Ask IBM and GM what good being in first place did for them.

9. Your flight has been delayed.

Everyone knows you should deliver more than you promised. What happens when you can't? Have the courtesy and the guts to give out the news as promptly, accurately, thoroughly, and honestly as possible. That creates trust. Delays and foulups are annoying, but tolerable. Lies and deceptions are not.

10. People don't plan to fail, they fail to plan. Worse yet, they fail to study the game films.

Yes, you've read this tip before in the section on negotiating. It applies to managing, too. Sure, what you do to prepare is important, but so is what you did while you were actually performing. Top negotiators, top athletes, top poker players debrief themselves after every major event. They always keep a book, not only on themselves, but on their opponents and every aspect of the event that affected the outcome.

Planning only tells you what you want to have happen. The postmortem tells you what actually happened.

In dealing with suppliers, most businesses are very demanding in drawing up specs and checking out competitors' prices and quality. That's called planning. But are they as exacting and rigorous in analyzing their own customers' reactions to the suppliers' products or services? That's a postperformance responsibility, and it is just as important to a business's bottom line.

MACKAY'S MORAL:

Lou Holtz said it: "Everyone wants to win on Saturday afternoon when the game is played. It's what you do the other six days that decides the outcome."

Chapter 55

FALLING UP

It's Friday afternoon. You, a manager, finally have taken the plunge and decided to fire Old Jimbo. We're not talking about "downsizing" or some other form of wholesale corporate homicide. This is the traditional one-on-one "I'm afraid you didn't live up to my expectations" termination of a veteran employee.

You call Old Jimbo into the office, shut the door, and tell him it's time to pack it in. Old Jimbo does not take it like a trooper. He's surprised. He's hurt. He's angry.

The fact is . . . it's all your fault.

Why? Because Old Jimbo didn't have a clue. At least not from anything you said to him.

How could he have known he didn't live up to your expectations unless you made it clear to him exactly what those expectations were, and how they may have changed with the inevitable shifts in corporate policies?

That's *your* job, not Old Jimbo's. Here we go again: Agreements prevent disagreements. A manager cannot arbitrarily raise the bar on an employee's performance. If there are to be new duties, upgraded skills, a better attitude, you must make them clear and monitor them closely. You must break out your best coaching moves and work with the individual. And if *all* your efforts fail, then and only then, should you suggest that person jump to another lily pad.

Spotting, hiring, and keeping winners is vital. So is cutting losers. The quality of your people is the most important element in building a successful business. In baseball, that quality is measured in fractions—fractions of a second and fractions of an inch. But those tiny fractions represent the difference between major league ball and pseudoball.

A while back I toured Redmond Products, a $120 million hair-products company. Redmond competes successfully with billion-dollar outfits like Helene Curtis, Alberto-Culver, and Procter & Gamble. At the end of the tour, I asked the CEO, Tom Redmond, whom they call "Coach," what differentiates his company from the competition.

"TGIM," said Redmond.

"What's that?"

"It stands for 'Thank God it's Monday.' "

"Attitude?"

"That's right. When our employees go home on Friday, I want them to feel they just can't wait to get back here on Monday. I'd like every one of them to really love what they're doing and not just work for a paycheck."

"How?"

"First, by hiring right. Second, by creating a work environment that's safe, clean, collegial, challenging, exciting, and rewarding. That's a big order. I'm never sure I've got it right, so I'm constantly tinkering with the formula. What makes it so damn much fun is I've got so many talented people to help me. Good people, clearly defined goals, endless improvements in how we reach those goals. That's the not-so-magic formula."

How can you be sure you hire right? You can't be. I've literally spent years stalking a candidate I want for a major hire, and then, after snaring my catch, discover within a few weeks that we've both made a mistake. But what I lack in hiring ability, I learned to make up in firing ability. This was a very long and difficult learning process, but I finally realized it was the people we didn't fire that made our lives miserable.

A major business publication asked executives to tell them about the toughest part of their jobs. The overwhelming majority responded that it was firing someone. They gave any number of reasons, most of which were of the guilty conscience variety: "We're talking about another living, breathing person here, with a family"; "As long as we're making money, I can't bring myself to cut someone off just for a few extra bucks." All very human, and understandable. And wrong. For both sides of the equation.

The irony is, in many cases, the company is actually doing the employee a favor.

Yes, I know the old story about Winston Churchill. In the elections held shortly after World War II, his party was soundly defeated. Attempting to soften the blow, Churchill's wife ventured that "Perhaps it was a blessing in disguise."

"If it is," said Churchill, "then it is most effectively disguised."

It was. He managed to land on his feet.

As did Ronald Reagan, Lee Iacocca, and Walt Disney, among others who got the axe.

As traumatic as it is, firing can be the one clear message that will convince a person to switch to something they're better at, rather than trying to hang on, hitting on one or two cylinders.

The most creative of all solutions may be to "fire" THE OLD YOU before someone has the incentive to do so. In his book *Only the Paranoid Survive*, Intel CEO Andrew Grove relates a pivotal incident in his and Intel's history. At that time Intel was dishing out research dough in three businesses, including memory chips and microprocessors. It didn't know which way to go. Grove says, "We were wandering in the valley of death." The company was taking a bath in memories. Intel inside was Intel in pain.

Intel had invented the microprocessor in 1970, but 15 years later many industry experts still couldn't grasp how microprocessors would revolutionize computing. Grove and his boss did. Of a 1985 meeting with Chairman and CEO Gordon Moore, then-president Grove recounts this exchange:

> "If we got kicked out and the board brought in a new CEO, what do you think he would do?" Gordon answered without hesitation, "He would get us out of

memories." I stared at him, numb, then said, "Why shouldn't you and I walk out the door, come back and do it ourselves?"

And so, with that, they did.

Did it work? You can bet your Pentium it did! They "fired" their old vision of themselves and, in doing so, created the dominant semiconductor firm in the world. Sometimes it's just a question of letting go of the past.

MACKAY'S MORAL:

A firing can be just what it takes to get you fired up.

Chapter 56

THE RETURN OF
THE NATIVE

It was Friday afternoon and the week was winding down. Our top sales executive slipped into my office, closed the door, sat down in the chair opposite my desk, and hit me over the head with a two-by-four.

"Harvey, I'm leaving you and going to work for XYZ Envelope [one of our major competitors]. They offered me a better deal, and I just can't turn it down."

For a nanosecond one overriding concern flashed through my mind: "Is this a capital punishment state or do they just give you life for murder?"

I resisted the impulse to lunge across the desk. The traditional farewell, "Clean out your desk and don't let the door hit you on the way out," welled up in my throat. I bit my tongue. Some oft-repeated parental wisdom filtered through the fog of anger: "In a crisis, a knee-jerk reaction is usually a just-plain-jerk reaction. Play it cool. You never want to burn your bridges unless you're a mighty good swimmer."

"Y'don't say?" I responded weakly. "Tell me about it." He told me the whole story from start to finish: how the initial contact had been made, what the offer was, why he had decided to accept it. I listened closely, got all the facts, and then said, "I'm asking for just one thing: Before I say anything substantive, and before you do anything further, let's sleep on it. We've been together too long and it's too important a decision to be set in concrete in one highly charged conversation. Let's meet again tomorrow."

We met again on Saturday. We'd both had time to think it over. I had spent Friday evening burning up the phone wires with people whose opinions I valued, trying to get every possible perspective I could on this bombshell before I went back onto the battlefield. By the time we sat down again, our emotions had quieted and we methodically analyzed the situation together. I was convinced that the move was a mistake from both our points of view. XYZ had promised him the moon. Big bonus . . . big title (president) . . . big T&E account . . . big bucks . . . long-term security. However, I knew the players on the other side better than he did and had virtually no confidence that they could deliver what they had promised. I brought up every negative I could think of, but I couldn't change his mind. He had stars in his eyes.

We parted amicably. Now here's where I went against the conventional wisdom.

"The door here is always open," I said. "I have a policy contrary to most of my peers. I don't believe in telling someone who has performed admirably in the past never to darken my door again. If things don't work out at your new shop, let's see if we can work things out again here."

As Paul Harvey would say, "Now here's the rest of the story."

After four years of bitter disappointments, severe recession, lack of capital, and a myriad of other problems, my former employee was knocked out of the box. The first thing I did when I learned he was out was to remind him of our open-door policy. I knew he'd be a better person after having had to face all that adversity.

He jumped at the offer and it worked out beautifully for both of us.

Of course, critics will jump all over me for doing this, saying "What a dummy Harvey is. All this does is encourage people to leave on a whim and know they can get their jobs back anytime they want them."

Not true.

Taking back employees after they've left depends on why they went. I'll rehire them if:

1. They were pirated away by a pie-in-the-sky competitor and it didn't work out,

2. They left to go into business for themselves and wound up in chapter 11,

3. They had a problem that caused me to terminate them and five years or so later they have proven they have the problem licked.

I have had real-life experience with each of these situations. I've never been sorry.

MACKAY'S MORAL:

Stay open . . . the second verse may be
better than the first.

Chapter 57

SPEED KILLS

The greatest trick in business is to create a breakthrough product category, like the computer.

The greatest trick in marketing is to convince people that they actually need it.

The computer has three basic strategic values: speed, cost effectiveness, and quality.

Three, not one. Three.

The problem is, there is too much emphasis on speed. Speed is a yardstick, a measurement. In and of itself, speed is a meaningless number. To have any business value, speed must serve a purpose.

I make envelopes. I buy high-speed envelope-making machines bristling with all sorts of computer gizmos. But sometimes, I wonder why.

Is it to get the envelopes to my customers faster? Yes, but if they are that desperate for an envelope, maybe a fax machine would do the job.

Is it to save money? Well, yes, but at a million bucks a pop, it takes a long, long time to recover your investment, and by then, they've got a $2 million machine all greased up and ready to go.

Why then? I'm afraid a lot of what I'm paying for is "We've-got-the-fastest-envelope-machine-in-the-upper-Mississippi-Watershed-District" bragging rights.

Marketing hype.

In pursuit of speed, we lose track of cost. While speed is infinite, the cost effectiveness of speed is finite. Going twice as fast may provide you with twice the cost benefit of your previous speed. But I can assure you that whatever it is you do, going a hundred times as fast does not assure you of 100 times the cost benefit. The faster you go, the less incremental cost benefit you receive.

Speed is glamorous. Cost accounting is dull. It's for people who carry their pens in a plastic sleeve in their front shirt pockets. And quality is for the old-timers in overalls who use hand tools, fine sandpaper, and camel's hair brushes.

The German magazine *Focus* ran an article titled "Race Without Victors." The subheading was "Always faster, always more expensive." Speed, as with any other virtue carried to an extreme, becomes a vice.

The last I read about it, the soothsayers were estimating that the cost of retooling America's computers for the millennium is going to run into the hundreds of billions of dollars.

No one seems to be asking if the money it costs will be worth the money it saves.

Bob Cratchit wouldn't even need to sharpen his nib to ramp up for January 1, 2000.

Almost every company I know is caught up in the speed game.

IBM used to eat everyone's lunch simply by waiting out their competitors' new products. After the inevitable recalls and failures, IBM used their giant marketing and service reputation to lurch in with their own products. It worked. Until they let the competition get too much of a lead and lap them, or literally, laptop them.

Customers have learned to accept products that are less than perfect, products that will be outmoded in six months, just to get the current speed advantage.

What is the purpose?

Virtually every manufacturing company in America is trying to bring their products to market faster and faster.

I repeat, what is the purpose?

When you're drawing your gun against Billy the Kid, speed matters.

In business, speed has no value for its own sake.

And as for quality, forget it.

Does anyone believe fast food is better than real food?

We're told that customers won't tolerate waiting four or five rings for the phone to be answered. The standard is three rings. Of course, when the three-ring cycle is completed, the three-ring circus starts. The phone is answered all right, but the customer is immediately put on hold while a disembodied voice informs him/her they will now be given an endless menu of number-coded options, "so we can serve you more quickly."

C'mon, is that an improvement in the quality of service?

And why do we want to talk to a real live person? To find out why last month's phone bill was $578,100 when it should have been $57.81.

Speed *can* provide a better way of doing business. But speed can also be nothing more than marketing hype.

MACKAY'S MORAL:

Don't get high on speed.

THE VALUE(S) OF YOUR ORGANIZATION

"Dilbert" notwithstanding, corporate mission statements, acronyms, and buzzwords are useful tools. Other cultures, like Japan, have gone even further and embellished them with company songs and cheers.

It's fun to make fun of them, but who can doubt the impact of *"Gung ho!" "Semper Fi,"* and "The Marine Hymn" on the morale of the U.S. Marines?

The military analogy applies to corporate cultures, because these shorthand expressions of institutional values really are a sort of battlecry, a means for employees to bond for a common purpose.

Values are meant to be costly. It if didn't cost much, we wouldn't appreciate the value.

You don't get to be a marine just by enlisting. You have to pay your dues. You have to earn the right to be part of the team.

Mackay Envelope Corporation does not resemble Quantico—I hope—but we have values we try to instill in our people.

Chicago department-store tycoon Marshall Field once indicated the following 12 reminders that can be helpful in obtaining a sound sense of values. These time-honored principles never change:

1. The value of time.
2. The success of perseverance.

3. The pleasure of working.
4. The dignity of simplicity.
5. The worth of character.
6. The power of kindness.
7. The influence of example.
8. The obligation of duty.
9. The wisdom of economy.
10. The virtue of patience.
11. The improvement of talent.
12. The joy of originating.

The mission statement for Mackay Envelope is: "To be in business forever."

Our employees know that translates into a single word: survival.

Not long ago the United States had 250 envelope companies. Now we're at 200, and we have yet to see any evidence that we're even stabilizing, much less trending upward again.

Hey, it may not be the Amazon, but we know that it's a jungle out there.

We value lots of things here: humor, honesty, fairness, the ability to get along with others, business judgment, product knowledge, motivation.

Most of all, we value results.

That's why we're still around to answer the roll call.

If I may refer to the marines again, it's similar to the reason they have boot camp. However, unlike the marines, nobody ever told their folks that when they grew up they wanted to be in the envelope business. So before we hire, we do a lot of screening, including psychological testing, checking and rechecking information, and endless interviews.

Recently, I hired a woman sales representative in the Chicago area. It takes me forever to hire any job prospect, but it's a lot better for all concerned. Better to lose a few by moving at a glacial pace than to make a hire on impulse that doesn't work out.

During my interview with Jane, I popped one of my favorite questions, "Jane, how many hours a week do you work?"

I was expecting a "sound barrier" number. Instead she blurted, "Oh, about 20 hours."

"Twenty hours? Wait a minute, what did you say your dollar volume was last year in Chicago?"

"$2 million."

"We can check, you know."

"So check. That's what I did, and I can do it for your company, too, and even better."

It checked. I hired her. I don't ask her how many hours she works. I don't care. This year her W2 form will be six figures.

Gung ho! Jane.

MACKAY'S MORAL:

Each organization has a unique culture. Identify it, distill it, share it, value it!

Chapter 59

THE ONE-WEEK MBA

Up through 1994, Hyatt Hotels more or less closed down their corporate offices for a week each year and the 100-plus executives scattered to their more than one hundred properties, which include some of the most lavish resort and vacation destinations that can be found anywhere.

Fun in the sun? Well, only if your idea of fun is making beds, washing dishes, and parking cars.

These hoteliers know that the best and only way to know what is going on in the trenches is to get in the trenches.

Let me make a modest suggestion, which I will immodestly dub the Mackay Corollary to the Hyatt Strategy. Any company smart enough to determine a major corporate policy by asking their salespeople what to do is going to be a winner.

Who is on the front lines dealing with customers every day?

The sales force.

Not the advertising geniuses, the financial wizards, the marketing gurus, the production magicians, or the executive leaders.

The people who know what the people who buy your products want and what they are willing to pay for them are the people who make their living selling those products. I have a short course designed for every CEO in America. It takes a week to complete. Some Monday morning plop yourself into the passenger seat of one of your middle-level salespeople, and start clocking windshield time. Midweek, switch to another salesperson in another region. If you're really ambitious, take the postgraduate course, switch again, and spend a few more days at it the following week. Here's what you'll learn:

1. You'll learn what your average salesperson knows about the company's overall goals and strategy, its product line, and the image it is trying to convey in the marketplace.

2. You'll learn what your average customer thinks about the company, its products, and its sales force; what the company's real image is in the marketplace.

3. You'll learn what your customers and your salespeople know about your competitors, and how those competitors are performing against you in the field.

4. You'll discover how well your average salesperson has been trained, what they know about the company's prospects and goals, whether they have set reasonable goals for themselves and have a reasonable plan for achieving their goals.

5. You'll see how your people negotiate and whether they're straight shooters. (You'll also find out who they scapegoat for quality and service defects.)

6. You'll learn if your people feel they have a stake in the business, or whether they regard themselves as order takers who are merely pawns of headquarters higher-ups (like you, for example).

7. You'll learn where your company's weaknesses are by observing where and what the salesperson has to give, in order to make a sale.

8. You'll learn what your people think of their sales managers, their level of compensation, what inroads are being made by the competition, the future of the industry, what changes are taking place in their customers' own

businesses, the weather, and the prospects for the Cowboys in the coming NFL season.

I guarantee you any CEO who takes the Mackay Windshield Admiration and Contemplation course will come back a better, smarter CEO. There's a side benefit, too. Word gets around. You cared enough to share major motel time with the road team. You can't measure the boost that will give to morale. Or rather, you can measure it. Wait until you see the next sales figures from the people you rode with. If you don't notice a spike, your next gross of envelopes is on me.

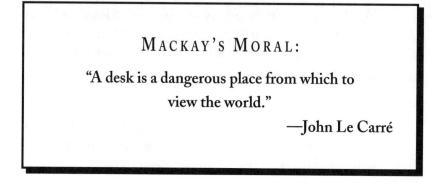

MACKAY'S MORAL:

"A desk is a dangerous place from which to
view the world."

—John Le Carré

Chapter 60

ONE-ON-ONE

This isn't a Harvey chapter. It's a Scott Mitchell chapter. Scott is president of Mackay Envelope Corporation. He reinstituted a program I started and dropped 10 years ago. We call it "One-on-One." On a regular basis, the president of the company gets out from behind his desk and calls on every employee individually, spending 20 to 30 minutes with each of them. That's 500 x 25 minutes, or approximately one solid month of a working year. Scott's rules are:

1. No rules. No holds barred. No repercussions. Let it all hang out.
2. I'll take notes, so people can be assured this is not a one-night stand, and there will be a basis for measuring results.
3. Repeat rule #1.

I want to share some of Scott's notes with you with one additional rule: no names and with the employees' okay.

Job	Years at Mackay	Comment
Printer	40	Meets with men's group every week to get things off his chest.
Printer	40	Lost his father in W.W.II. Is proud to work here.
Printer	36	One of the first people to play golf on the back nine of Rich

		Acres. Very involved with the handicapped. Had to feed and dress her sister until she was 16.
Shipping	34	Ran the roller coaster at an amusement park. While waiting for an ambulance, he gave his best shirt to a guy who fell head first through the tracks.
Cutting	34	Really thinks we need a formalized maintenance program. He's right.
Adjuster	33	Makes photo mugs and has a proprietary machine. I had him talk to ——— about photo trade shows. He once had a bad attitude. Doesn't now.
Stock Handler	31	A tree hugger. Would never leave Mackay because he remembers filling out hundreds of applications 33 years ago.
Janitor	30	Now a janitor after spending 29 years on the bailer. Cost him $200 to get his job with Mackay 30 years ago and would do it all over again.
Adjuster	28	Feels that quality should be in the hands of adjuster and operator. Doesn't like people checking his work. We discussed quality and that we should measure it by customer's perception.
Shipping	26	Feels people should stay over their shift to give a hand. She says we need more cartons.

Adjuster	26	Thinks the best operators are ——— and ———. Likes ———, too. His favorite movie is *It's a Mad, Mad, Mad, Mad World*.
Sheeter	26	One of seven boys and one girl. Raised six kids. Goes hunting and fishing every weekend. Feels shipping is having trouble keeping track of what's coming in.
Adjuster	26	While making a delivery, met Hubert Humphrey in his underwear.
Printer	15	Lost five brothers in the French takeover of Vietnam. Later escaped the Communists.
Adjuster	15	Maintenance department is farming out too many jobs that adjusters could do when not busy.

There's lots more. "Move the first aid box." "Needs a new handjack." "The third-shift supervisor should have a key to the tools." But that's not the stuff that makes my eyes mist over. Anybody who thinks a job is just a job has only to spend a few minutes with Scott's notes to see people with real lives jump out everywhere. I don't think I have to tell you it works, or that I was an idiot for having discontinued it when I thought we had gotten "too big" for me to meet with every employee. Maybe I had just gotten "too big." I'm glad Scott hasn't.

MACKAY'S MORAL:

Faxes and voice mail are modern and fine,
But not worth a damn versus knowing the line.
If sales go bust and it looks like you'll flop,
You'll learn the truth first from the folks in the shop.

Chapter 61

THE BOAT WON'T GO IF WE ALL DON'T ROW

The fabled Chicago Cubs double-play combo of Tinkers to Evers to Chance all hated each other. Okay, so every now and then people who don't like the people they work with combine to put together an outstanding performance.

That's man bites dog. Everyone expects a bunch of winners to get along with each other, and since that's almost always what happens, it's not news when they do. Rarely does a group of unhappy people achieve success, and I have rarely seen a company with happy employees that was not successful.

Companies that concentrate just on satisfying their customers and whipping competition to a pulp miss the easiest audience of all: their own employees. Focus on them, and the rewards are huge.

Here's how.

1. Build team morale.

At the top of my list of hiring criteria is a manager's ability to inject a sense of fun into the daily grind. In a glamour patch like publishing and theater and fashion, the work is its own reward. But when you're building envelopes, it's pretty hard for workers to visualize themselves on the cutting edge of creativity. Smart managers have been known to close down the shop for an afternoon and take everyone to the ball game; call out for pizza on the house; never forget a birthday (everyone takes a break for cake, ice cream, bad singing, and a gag gift);

and an unexpected bonus—in cash—for performance above and beyond the call of duty. The feeling that "we're all family" bonds the members of the team in a way nothing else does.

2. Listen to your team.

Don't think that thinking is the exclusive prerogative of management. Everyone has ideas about how their own job can be done better. And a few employees, not necessarily management types, will have good ideas about how the whole company can be improved.

Success is about thinking, not just working. Tactical skills can get you through the day, but they won't help you plan for tomorrow. There's a place for those who never miss a deadline or muff an assignment. But there's a bigger place for those who can tell you what the assignment is going to be a year from now. Thinking is the hardest, most valuable task any person performs. Don't stifle it . . . encourage it.

At Mackay Envelope we try to generate thinking by encouraging it and rewarding it. Seminars, conventions, advanced educational opportunities, bonuses, promotions, recognition in the house newsletter, press releases, contests. They're all tried-and-true devices and they all work and they all tell your employees you're paying attention to them.

Mistakes? Every company makes them. Ford had the Edsel. Coke almost abandoned its franchise product. IBM overemphasized mainframes. But that's all part of the game. You'll never stub your toe if you walk backwards, but you'll always be moving in the wrong direction. Better to take an occasional wrong turn. Vince Lombardi got it right when he said, "If you learn from a mistake, it really wasn't a mistake after all."

3. Hold team meetings.

At Mackay we have regular informational meetings. Sometimes we bring in speakers. Sometimes we use homegrown talent. We have book reports. Each sales meeting is kicked off with a funny story or joke on a rotational basis. One time we may emphasize sales. Another time, financial results. After we play Minneapolis, we take our dog and pony show to our Iowa facility. The bonding that takes place when we go on the road is one of the real benefits of the program. Sometimes I even make the traveling squad myself.

4. Build teams within the team.

General Electric has all but eliminated the traditional approach of passing along a project from one giant department to the next with myriad sign-offs and modifications up and down the bureaucratic ladder.

GE cuts through the red tape to assemble small interdepartmental working groups representing all the skills needed to develop, design, manufacture, finance, and market a product. The "small company within the big company" approach gets GE products to the marketplace faster and at less expense. It also shows GE's confidence in team members' abilities to solve multifaceted problems regardless of their job titles or nominal levels of authority.

How do you build cooperation among workers? There are any number of programs, like Outward Bound, that are designed to help managers break down the barriers and recognize the interdependent nature of teams.

I highly recommend the Minneapolis-based Pecos River, founded by Larry Wilson. His company helps organizations gain committed workers at a time when most experts would say employee loyalty and commitment is no longer possible.

Try one of these organizations. It will help make your team stronger.

MACKAY'S MORAL:

Team up. Make the company you keep keep your company strong.

Chapter 62

TOWARD A DEFINITION OF LEADERSHIP

I always thought of leadership as the art of determining whether they're chasing you or following you. Professor Ronald Heifetz, who lectures on leadership at Harvard's Kennedy School of Government, probably wouldn't agree, as indicated by the title of his book, *Leadership Without Easy Answers*.

What is leadership?

Let's start with what it isn't.

Leadership is not authority. Authority is compelled obedience. Authority is "The workday begins at 8:30 A.M. You are expected to be on time."

Leadership requires persuasion. You follow, not because you have to, but because you want to.

When Dwight Eisenhower was still a general, he used to demonstrate how to exercise leadership with a piece of string. He'd put it on his desk and push it, and of course, the string would crumple up. Then he would pull it, and the string would follow.

Corporate executives often confuse leadership with authority. It's an error of convenience. It certainly requires a lot less effort to tell someone what to do than to inspire them to do it. Why bother to fire up the troops when you can just fire the troops?

"The point is, leadership requires assessment of social dynamics as they are happening, in order to take corrective action with the next move," Heifetz is quoted in a recent article in *Harvard Magazine*.

In other words, able leaders are not just "Lone Rangers with vision." They are tactical as well as strategic masters. They create scenarios that persuade others to follow them.

Martin Luther King Jr. began a voting rights march in Selma, Alabama, because he knew that this was one of the places in the country where the civil authorities would be certain to assault the marchers with dogs and billy clubs. When they did, the conscience of the nation was shocked, and Congress was compelled to pass civil rights legislation.

Leadership is not just knowing what you stand for, but what you're willing to stand up against.

Heifetz contrasts this type of leadership with George Bush's war on drugs. Instead of trying to inspire others to join the cause, Bush took the traditional, "top-down, follow me," approach. He had General Noriega arrested, appointed William Bennett as his "drug czar," and got him $9 billion to use to end drug abuse.

Result: Drug abuse became worse than ever. By saying, in effect, "I'll take care of it," Bush never convinced us *we* had a problem. *He* had the problem. Sound strategy. Weak tactics.

Let's make it bipartisan and take the semimandatory shot at the Clintons' health care reform proposals a few years back. Unlike Bush, the Clintons were able to engage broad popular support and involvement in the program. Unfortunately, the program itself was flawed. What was "universal health care"? Was it "90 percent coverage"? "100 percent coverage"? Bill kept shifting the goal line and Hillary kept shifting it back, until no one understood what the administration stood for. Sound tactics. Weak strategy.

In the same issue of *Harvard Magazine*, an unrelated anecdote appears concerning another president. In 1930 Franklin Roosevelt, a Harvard grad, received a letter in which the signer identified himself as "Secretary of the Lowell House

Committee" and asked Roosevelt's permission to name the carillon of bells in Lowell House, Roosevelt's old dorm, the "Franklin Delano Roosevelt Bells." Roosevelt replied graciously that he would be delighted. Soon after, Julian Coolidge, the master of Lowell House, who had also been FDR's prep school mathematics teacher, caught wind of the matter. He wrote Roosevelt that he had been the victim of a "piece of undergraduate pleasantry." He also reminded his old pupil, "I have naturally attributed your present success to the mathematics you learned from me 35 years back."

Roosevelt was not unduly offended by the ruse. He wrote back,

> Dear Julian:
>
> I am not the least perturbed about the chime of bells, because, strictly between ourselves, I should much prefer to have a puppy dog or baby named after me than one of those carillon effects that is never quite in tune and which goes off at all hours of the day and night . . .
>
> Referring to the mathematics days, do you remember your first day's class at Groton? You stood up at the blackboard, announced to the class that a straight line is the shortest distance between two points, and then tried to draw one. All I can say is that I, too, have never been able to draw a straight line. I am sure you shared my joy when Einstein proved there ain't no such thing as a straight line!
>
> As ever yours,
> Franklin D. Roosevelt

There was a leader. A bit of charm never hurts, either.

MACKAY'S MORAL:

Leadership does not mean getting people to do their job. It means getting people to do their best.

RACING THE PONY EXPRESS

Chapter 63

MYTHS OF THE MARKETPLACE

1. We don't have any competition.

This is the attitude that practically sank IBM, General Motors, Schwinn bikes, and every other company that thought they could disregard and/or abuse their customers endlessly because their products were unique and indispensable. Surprise! They weren't. Every business, every individual, has competition. The more you act like you don't, the sooner you are to get it, and the tougher it's likely to be.

2. Downsizing is going to get rid of a lot of dead wood and enhance the profitability of the companies that engage in it.

The standard drill for a company that is downsizing is to comb the ranks for volunteers before ordering involuntary departures. Who is most likely to jump overboard in return for augmented severance benefits? It's not the seat warmers. It's the people who are best equipped to land on their feet somewhere else—with your competition, for instance—because they're the most capable, talented members of your work force. Who's going to hang on for dear life? Obviously, it's the marginal types and those who would have trouble finding a job somewhere else. The law of adverse selection is at work here. As in insurance, those who most want protection are those who need it the most.

Also, sawing off limbs may be effective therapy, but it is not a sign of good health. Recklessly trimming employees means trimming revenues and market share. Companies grow by increasing revenues and market share. Don't confuse a short-term survival tactic with a long-term growth strategy.

In fact, there's a new buzzword that's popped up called "dumbsizing." There's a reason. A study was made of 100 companies who had downsized thousands of their employees. One year later, these same companies were revisited and guess what? Same dumb companies! 35 percent of the companies' bottom lines were the same as before the downsizing occurred, still drowning in red ink.

3. Always be nice.

Always be nice as long as you can, and when you can't be nice anymore, do what you have to do. Hard looks, screaming, and jumping up and down may not win you any Boss of the Year awards, but they can be most effective as wake-up calls for the objects of the exercise. We all know that most of the big cigars didn't get where they got on charm alone.

Still, there are certain rules of conduct, even tough conduct, that should be followed. Never chew out a subordinate in front of anyone else unless it's an official termination and you want to make a record for legal purposes. In that case, you're not going to go ballistic anyway, unless you like lawsuits. We're talking about the ordinary, garden-variety flogging. When a third party is present when you lose your temper you have made it impossible for the floggee to save face and to correct their mistakes. Do it in private. You know what was said. They know what was said. That's enough. (But keep notes. It's a litigious age we live in).

4. The customer is always right.

The most revered aphorism of them all. How can I disagree? Well, the customer is usually right, but the one area where you have to be especially careful is in marketing. The reason something like 12 out of 13 new products flop isn't because marketers haven't tried hard to listen to their customers. It's because customers often don't have the interest to really focus on your marvelous new gizmo or improvement. Simply put, customers favor the familiar. As a result, they tend to give high marks to the knock-off that is familiar and easy to understand and shy away from the real breakthroughs. Can you imagine the reaction of the first focus group that was handed a pizza? I mean, who needs this gooey, oily thing when we already have toasted Velveeta-and-tomato sandwiches on Wonder bread? Or the fax machine? Who needs it? We have letters. We have phones. We have messengers. There comes a time when you have to go with your gut. You're paid for being right, not just for asking someone else whether you are or not.

MACKAY'S MORAL:

Popular wisdom is a contradiction in terms. If it's popular, it's popular, but it isn't wisdom. Wisdom involves seeing beyond what is popular.

Chapter 64

IN SUPPLY AND DEMAND, SUPPLY COMES FIRST

At our shop, getting and keeping suppliers is on a par with getting and keeping customers. Whoever it is you're in business *with* will do more, a lot more, to determine your success than the business you are *in*.

Make no mistake about it, you're in business with your suppliers. They are your lifeline to your customers. If that lifeline is unreliable, it doesn't matter how wonderful everything else is, your ship is dead in the water.

When I bought the bucket of nuts and bolts that was laughingly thought to be an envelope factory, my first move was to visit all the outfit's old suppliers. I explained I was new, young, inexperienced, but one thing I did know was that I couldn't make it without them.

"Sonny," they said, "we can sure see that, but that's your problem. The question is, how are you going to pay for the stuff?"

I produced letters of credit from my bank guaranteeing payment. As my suppliers, they would have zero risk. "Now that your question is answered," I said, "here's mine. Before I choose you as a supplier, how can I be sure you are going to be a reliable, competitively priced, high-quality supplier, who can meet my needs not only on a routine basis, but on an extra-effort basis during peak periods?"

Believe me, that little exchange of pleasantries got results. Fewer suppliers, but better suppliers. We had an understanding. I wanted suppliers who would be part of a long-range plan. They would count on me if I could count on them. But before we said our vows, I wanted to be sure they were going to be there for me when I needed them.

Good suppliers, like good customers, can last a lifetime. But like good customers, it's a relationship, not just a series of transactions. Relationships require constant monitoring, feedback, communication, and fine-tuning.

In the last few years the trend toward cutting down on the number of suppliers has been accelerating. The fewer the suppliers you work with, the more important are those remaining. Here are some things to consider:

- You need suppliers you can trust. You can't select suppliers intelligently if you don't have a clear understanding of your own goals, your standards for price, quality, reliability, and the need for peak performance at crunch times. In other words, you need *(a)* a strategic plan, *(b)* suppliers with whom you cannot only share your strategic plan, but who have *(c)* a strategic plan of their own that meshes with yours.

- You need suppliers who trust you. You have to know as much about their operations as you do about your own. You should know the top management of your suppliers. Do they have depth in talent and experience? Is it stable or susceptible to turnover? Is their vision of the future secure, or are they in flux, waiting to be sold?

- You need suppliers who can perform, not just today, but tomorrow. What is their skill set? Do they have the

capacity to grow with you, both in volume and in technological capability?

- You need suppliers who are part of the team, not part of
the problem. "Petty." "Aggravating." "Annoying." "Penny-
ante." If any of these words apply to the relationship, you
need new suppliers. Life's too short to spend it dealing
with stupid little hassles day in and day out.

MACKAY'S MORAL:

Your suppliers are your partners in business.
Choose them as carefully as you would choose
your partners in life.

In Care
of Others

Chapter 65

SECOND OPINIONS

There's a cautionary tale in *Smart Money* magazine about a lawyer named Judah Harris, who managed to lose $670,000 in the stock market over the last decade. It wasn't easy.

While Harris was going over the cliff, we were experiencing the greatest bull market in history. Obviously, Harris's investment strategy was flawed. He overtraded. He invariably sold his winners too soon and clung to his losers too long. He made investment decisions on the basis of rumors and tips he picked up in the public press, long after they had been reflected in the price of the stocks. Did I say "stocks"? This one-man black hole of investing gravitated to speculative, highly leveraged, time-sensitive derivatives known as "puts" and "calls" that amounted to little more than bets on the short-term direction of the market. He made the same amateurish mistakes over and over, the kind of mistakes that are flagged in all the "how to" books on investing.

Yet he made one mistake that I've rarely seen mentioned in the how-to manuals. Underlying his trading was a character trait that all but assured his downfall: He never discussed his investment decisions with his wife.

I am not about to use this book to tout the "Little Woman" theory of investment survival. But I will state that if you are your average macho male and if, when you take an honest look at your track record, it reveals that you are a less-than-astute investor, it's time to call in your partner for a consultation. Why do I address this to men? Because in my experience women do tend to consult their spouses on investment decisions. They don't need any prodding from me. Men go it alone. Macho time. It's a culture thing.

Eddie Albert has been a good family friend for many years. His is one of the most recognizable faces in the world, thanks to starring in *Green Acres*, a long-running television series. Eddie had the good fortune to have gained some entrepreneurial experience before he started making it as an actor. After serving in combat in World War II as a naval officer in the Pacific, he left the navy and established Eddie Albert Productions, an outfit that specialized in "industrials," business training films. Though his principal occupation has been acting, he's had a hand in business ever since. When I asked him what was the best business decision of his life, I had barely finished the sentence when he said "Margo . . . [his wife of over 40 years, who died some years ago] Margo was my advisor. I would take her advice on any deal that came across my desk.

"Money scared the hell out of me. I didn't know what to do with it. So until Margo came along I got rid of it as fast as I could," said Eddie. "You've heard of the Eddie Albert Miniature Golf Course? No? Well, let me know if you do, because I've got a pile invested in it and I've never been able to find the damn thing. I was known as Easy Eddie. I'm the kind of guy who would take the deals Burt Reynolds, Mickey Rooney, and Joe Louis all turned down.

"Whatever business training I had taught me one thing: I was no businessman. I was an actor who was fortunate enough to make enough money acting so I had some left over to invest. I needed help. So I turned to the person who had the biggest stake in my success, my wife. The only thing that's saved me since she's gone is the fact I'm getting a little hard of hearing. It's easier to say no when you can't hear the sizzle on the steak they're trying to sell you."

Eddie Albert is one of a long line of actors who've managed to hang on to what they had because they had shrewd wives.

Few stories of spousal second-opinion support can rival that recounted by actor Christopher Reeve in his autobiography *Still*

Me. Right after Reeve had his catastrophic riding accident in 1995, his wife, Dana, had to anticipate the press onslaught. She demanded that the doctors review Reeve's condition completely with him and made it clear nothing would be done without his consent.

When Reeve's own mother heard his survival chances were slim, Reeve says she became deeply agitated and advocated his doctors should "pull the plug." Dana insisted that decision be left up to Reeve. Without his being aware of it, his wife was there to offer a second opinion that proved decisive.

The next time you have an investment brainstorm or you are thinking about how you want to structure your medical power of attorney, don't keep it a secret. Get a second opinion from someone close to you. You'll always get points for asking. And, who knows, you might just learn something.

I've tried not to mouth the cliche "Two heads are better than one," but there it is. It generally helps to have a couple of people kick an idea around.

MACKAY'S MORAL:

Even the Lone Ranger didn't go it alone.

Chapter 66

7 THINGS NOT TO DO WITH A FRIEND

Someone once asked a great philosopher which he would rather have—a gift of money or a gift of friendship. "Friendship," replied the philosopher, "because money is spent but friendship can last forever."

"I shall think of that advice forever," the questioner responded, "as a mark of your friendship."

"Sorry," the philosopher apologized, "my friendship is free, but my advice isn't. Pay up."

As you will see in this chapter, money is but one of the ways to lose friends.

1. Go into business with . . .

George has been your personal friend forever. You do everything together. So you and George become business partners. A few months into this grand alliance, a few chinks appear. It turns out that George's work habits are a bit different from yours.

You're an early riser. George thinks early is anything that happens before noon. You've put in four hours before George puts in an appearance. You're a detail person. George can't be bothered with the fine print; he's a charmer. That can be just dandy, if your Mr. Inside/Mr. Outside arrangement is viable. But even though George is handling sales to take advantage of his people skills, you're in a business where your customers still carry slide rules and want everything done by the numbers. George no can do. What can you do?

2. Buy something from . . .

You're finally going to add that three-season porch your spouse has been wanting for the last 23 seasons. Good Old Ollie's just getting started in the remodeling business. Why not let him do it? Though G.O.O.'s bid is 25 percent higher than anyone else's, he assures you that "you get what you pay for." He must have meant leaks and broken tiles. You can't very well turn him into the Better Business Bureau, so you just bite the bullet while someone else fixes Ollie's follies.

3. Sell something to . . . (reverse of 2.)

Your dad goes into a nursing home. He has a three-year-old car with very low mileage. You were going to advertise it, but your friend Sid pesters you to sell it to him. You do, and take a $500 haircut. Then after three months the transmission goes out. Sid seems to think that's something you should pay for. Funny, you and Sid don't get together as much anymore.

4. Hire . . .

Friend Ralph worked for a Fortune 500 company and says he was downsized out of a job. He's an accountant, and you have a serious bean-counting deficiency. A marriage made in heaven? Not quite. You discover that the corporation that canned Ralph may have been onto something more than just a routine restructuring. It seems that learning new ways to do things is not to be found on Ralph's balance sheet. You never bothered to check him out, of course, because this is a guy you'd known for 20 years. Too bad, because after six months Ralph "doesn't work here anymore."

5. Go to work for . . . (reverse of 4.)

You took early retirement and decided to go to work for your old fraternity brother Alex, a self-made zillionaire who was two years ahead of you in college. Boy, Alex was a real wild man in those days. Unfortunately, he still is. He screams. He curses. He harasses. Alex thinks it's still Hell Week and he has the paddle. You depledge.

6. Go on an extended trip with . . .

Greg and Lisa are great company, so this long vacation with them would be a guaranteed blast. Well, it was a "blast" as in "explosion" or "bomb." You've always been a generous tipper. Not Greg. He'd stiff any waiter or waitress if he had the chance. It used to seem kind of cute, but not anymore, not when it got repeated over and over, every day, every meal. No amount of nudging or teasing seemed to work. Toward the end of the trip, you'd have to sneak back to the table and throw down a couple extra bucks to make up for Greg's cheapness. And no bill was ever split 50/50. Greg always found a way to shave a few pennies off his end. Punctuality wasn't one of Greg's virtues either. Every day you'd wait for them in the lobby before you could get going. Little things? Oh yeah. But they sure can get big in a hurry.

7. Lend to or borrow money from . . .

All of the above problems are minor compared to this one. More friendships have been trashed because of money than all the other reasons combined. Do your banking with a banker.

MACKAY'S MORAL:

Friends are made by many acts . . . and lost by only one.

Chapter 67

HOW TO PICK
AN EXPERT

Did you ever wonder what happens to people who win the lottery? Lois won $176,000 and wrote a letter about it to the *St. Paul Pioneer Press*.

After she paid her taxes and some bills, she had about $100,000 left. She and her husband got new cars, bought a cabin, and invested in a fourplex. Seems like pretty normal behavior to me, but let Lois tell us what happened next:

"The dealer took advantage of us, the cabin needed new wiring, the fourplex has a leaky basement. We're up to our neck in bills. I wish we'd never won."

If you suddenly find yourself sitting on an unexpected pile of money, say from an inheritance or an IRA rollover, would you know what to do?

Nice problem, but with the Lois example still fresh in your mind, you're aware it's still a problem. You don't want to have to act on a crisis basis, the surest way to mess up.

It won't happen if you're prepared.

The way to prepare is the same way you get to Carnegie Hall: Practice, practice, practice. And pretend a lot.

Over the years you have invested small sums, making believe they were large ones. Sure, it wasn't a lot of money, and you experienced varying degrees of success. Some were rank speculations. Some were conservative. Some of the people with whom you have invested have been duds. Others have been trustworthy, have earned your confidence, and have produced results. These are your experts.

Maybe they are individuals. Maybe they are institutions. Whatever the case, they have provided you with advice, you made some significant decisions based on that advice, and now your potential experts have established a track record you can use to help you make even more significant decisions.

You can use this process in almost any situation you may encounter. Suppose you're considering a midcareer move to a new profession, another company, or another corner of the world? How do you prepare? Practice. Start taking courses. Subscribe to the trade magazines. Get company publications. Check out the local papers. And most important of all, use these leads—the instructors, the authors and subjects of the articles you have read—to start making personal contacts.

You're going to get some surprises, because you can never tell who will come through for you. The nice surprise is, some people will.

Here are four points to remember in picking an expert:

- **Go to someone you already know and trust.** When a problem hits is a lousy time to look for someone you can trust. How can you know you can depend on someone you've known for half an hour? I would rather rely on someone I knew I could count on, even if their experience were limited, than the charming stranger with the pinkie ring I met last week at a backyard barbecue.

- **Use an expert to find another expert in the same profession.** Don't ask a lawyer to help you pick a doctor.

- **Be prepared to pay for any advice you get.** Even when all you are asking your first expert to do is recommend a second expert. Compensation puts expert number one all the more on the line in making a solid recommendation.

- **Don't be afraid to ask questions . . . a lot of them.** One of my favorite investment probes is "Are you putting your own money in the investment that you are recommending to me?"

There must be something vaguely unhealthy about this question, because you'd be surprised how many coughing fits it generates. I don't insist that my expert share the risk with me, but if I get an obvious lie in response to this question, or any other, I back off. The general principle is: faithless in one thing, faithless in all. Another classic, "How much are you being paid to provide me this service (give me this advice)?"

There are also a couple of benefits from this experience that are rarely noted.

You have added to your own self-confidence and expertise by making a decision in a tough situation, based upon incomplete or even conflicting advice.

Most important of all, whether you ever find yourself in this situation, you have engaged in one of the most useful exercises you will ever experience. Why? Because throughout life most of our preparations are for disasters, not for success. What happens the first day at school? Fire drill. Who's the first person to show up at the door when we get back from the honeymoon? The life insurance salesperson. Don't just fantasize about success, prepare for it. It's the surest route there is to achieving it.

MACKAY'S MORAL:

The key to finding an expert is: Dig your well before you're thirsty. (Where have I heard that line before?)

Chapter 68

HOW TO PICK AN EXPERT II

How do you tell when an expert isn't?

No system is foolproof.

Michael Cimino, who made the Academy Award winner *The Deer Hunter*, also made the world-class stinker *Heaven's Gate*.

If one set of experts can blow $36 million betting on the talents of another expert, then we are all at risk. There seem to be a lot more horror stories in circulation than there are solutions, but let's take a crack at some answers.

As we mentioned previously, there's the Be Prepared method. You keep testing various experts over the years with small assignments, getting yourself in shape for the day when the real thing comes along.

Okay, you're like most people. You didn't prepare. You unexpectedly inherited a pile from your Uncle Fudd, who always thought you were a cute little bugger.

Spread the risk. You don't have an expert. So get five experts. All at once. That's what many major institutions do with their endowments. They hire several investment managers, start them each with small amounts, see how they do, and over the years weed out the weak performers and give more responsibility to the successful ones.

The idea has spread to medical care, too. I'm not just referring to the standard drill of "getting a second opinion." Medical insurance companies and HMOs use an "outcomes-oriented" method to select care providers. They compile exhaustive statistical records on medical case histories, comparing doctors on the basis of the results each achieved among patients with similar medical problems. Those care providers who deliver the best outcomes in patient care at the lowest cost make the cut. Those that don't are dropped from the approved list, or are reimbursed at a lower level than the more cost-effective doctors.

Blindingly simple. It's the difference between a negotiated contract between one buyer and one seller and changing the equation, still one buyer, but only a portion of the contract going to each seller. The twist here is, no one gets the contract, not all of it, anyway, so the competition between suppliers, the experts, doesn't end when the contract is awarded. They keep on competing, as long as the company wants the component or service.

Okay, you weren't prepared, you didn't spread the risk, and now you want to be sure the expert you are thinking of hiring can perform. Let's say you need to hire an advertising agency and you haven't spent a lifetime researching advertising agencies. How do you hire grown people who go to work in jeans, when everybody else you have ever hired comes to work in a suit? You've heard their pitch and of course, it's impressive, but it's their own stuff. How do you decide?

Check those references. I don't mean just *present* clients, I mean *previous* clients. Get those names. It's very simple. Just ask, "Will you furnish me with the names of all your previous clients over the past five years?" A no is an automatic out, like an undisclosed prior felony.

Why this insistence on previous clients? Because all a present client is ever going to tell you is just what the folks standing in front of you in suits will tell you: what's going right.

You want to know what can go wrong.

Only a departed client is going to tell you that. Is it billing? Service? Quality of the creative work? Loyalty? You want to know why clients leave, because if it happened to them, it can happen to you. It's the equivalent of a Frequency of Repair record on a particular model of car. When you sign up with these guys, what causes breakdowns?

There's another question I always ask, and it's wilted more smiles on hucksters' faces than the sales manager telling them "We're cutting your territory."

"Who," I ask innocently, "is going to be assigned responsibility for this account on a day-to-day basis?"

If it isn't the person who made the pitch, I tune out immediately.

The key to picking an expert is reaching over the suits and getting one-on-one with the grunts who are actually doing the work. If I am asking for expert advice in constructing an investment portfolio, I don't want an account man to interpret for me to the securities analyst. I want the securities analyst. We both speak the mother tongue. If I am trying to pick an advertising agency, I want the copywriter and the art director to hear the sound of my voice as I describe our typical customer, and I want to eyeball them, hear the sound of theirs, and see their individual portfolios.

Primitive, this insistence of mine on human contact in selecting the people upon whom my life or personal fortune may depend. But it is a privilege I demand when I am spending my money, and so should you.

MACKAY'S MORAL:

The people you're dealing with when you're picking an expert are usually all experts. The question is: Are they expert at selling it, or are they expert at doing it?

Chapter 69

IN GENERAL, WE PREFER LEADERSHIP

We sure like generals. If Colin Powell were to be elected, he'd be the tenth general to be president.

Only three generals never held public office prior to the presidency: Taylor, Grant, and Eisenhower.

Despite experience in office, three were still much better known at the time of their elections for their military rather than their political leadership: Washington, Jackson, and William Henry Harrison.

Three, Benjamin Harrison, Hayes, and Garfield, all Civil War generals, were more or less professional politicians when they were elected.

Turning to military leaders for civilian leadership is an American tradition. In several cases, the results have been spectacular. In others, they are far from it.

Why do we do it?

Because we want leadership, and generals are professional leaders.

If we look beyond the gold braid and the famous victories, what are the qualities that make for leadership?

And keep in mind, leaders are not just generals, presidents, and CEOs. We're all leaders. We lead families, and we lead teams at work.

Marshall Loeb, the editor-at-large of *Fortune* magazine, spoke recently on "Ten Steps to Effective Leadership." I've paraphrased his words and changed them a bit, but the major points are Loeb's. Don't blame him for the finger-pointing. Most of that is mine.

1. Leading is not managing. The late Grace Hopper, the first woman admiral in the United States Navy, said, "You manage things, but you lead people." A manager wants to be liked. A leader wants to be respected.

2. Leaders have a sense of purpose. They think in terms of achieving goals, or as the world's number-one goal achiever, Wayne Gretzky, puts it, "It's not where the puck *is* that counts. It's where the puck *will be*." In other words, leaders have that sense of where the culture is going to be . . . where the organization must be if it is to grow.

3. Leaders have courage. They make the tough calls. Lincoln fought a war rather than let the Union dissolve; he stuck with Grant, who took a lot of casualties, rather than the popular—and cautious—McClellan. His decision to free the slaves was popular mainly with the slaves—and they didn't have the vote. Like Lincoln 80 years before him, Harry Truman is also a lot more popular today than when he left the presidency—with a 32 percent approval rating.

4. Leaders are forceful. They have a point of view, and they express it clearly. You don't have to guess where they stand.

5. Leaders are consistent. They inspire trust and confidence because they don't change horses—or courses—in midstream. Loeb cites the CEO of American Express, Harvey Golub, who says that he has discovered that when he's tired of repeating the same message over and over, it means he probably has reached the

point where his people finally understand it. Why fight hard for the leader's program if you can't count on the leader to stick with it?

6. Leaders are truthful. Even when it hurts. Kennedy took the rap for the Bay of Pigs. Nixon stonewalled and deceived on Watergate. Followers accept honest mistakes. They don't accept lies and cover-ups.

7. Leaders concentrate on a couple of big themes; they don't try to do it all. President Carter had a fine, logical mind, but he got stuck on the details. Reagan couldn't remember a detail to save his life. He succeeded as a leader because he stayed with his program and kept it short and simple.

8. Leaders don't have to pretend they thought of everything themselves. They aren't afraid to make use of other people's ideas. The Japanese didn't invent the assembly line, but they took over global leadership of the car industry (for a while) by studying and then refining American methods.

9. Leaders are made, not born. They have climbed over obstacles that have held back lesser people. Their personal histories are as inspirational as their achievements are measurable. One thing leaders have in common, they all have followers.

10. How do you spot a leader? Look at the people around the leader. Are they hacks and gofers? Or are they achievers, people with talent and good moral character, people who can stand as leaders in their own right? Leaders are not threatened by being surrounded by people of quality; they are energized by them.

MACKAY'S MORAL:

We elect a general for president when leadership
matters more to us than ideology.

Chapter 70

IF YOU ASK FOR HELP . . . ASK THE RIGHT PERSON

There are certain ways of earning a living in this country that are kind of tough to warm up to. "Hi, I'm Elmo, and I'm a used car salesman." ". . . vice cop." ". . . repo man." (Okay, "collection agent.")

Hopefully "envelope peddler" doesn't fit in this category. I'm too close to that game to be objective, but I'll have to admit they don't play "Hail to the Chief" when I tell folks that's what I do for a living.

"Consultant" is another tarnished career description, more so in recent years now that so many people have been downsized into consulting rather than choosing it voluntarily.

Too bad, because consultants receive a bum rap; they're invaluable. The ones with advanced degrees are called lawyers, doctors, professors, industrial psychologists, and engineers. We don't think of them as consultants, but often they are. We hire them just to give us advice in broad terms rather than to strut their stuff with the instruments of their profession.

I have used consultants all my life, and here's my take on consulting: Most consultants enjoyed some measure of success early in their careers. The reputations they gained from those early triumphs enabled them to survive professionally. However, times change, and so do the formulas for achieving results.

In my experience, too many consultants tend to apply the same solution to every problem. They tend to rest on their laurels. They haven't grown.

That's "most," not "all," and that just represents my own experience. It's only anecdotal evidence, hardly a scientific survey. If I were to quantify it, I'd say 70 percent of the consultants out there are sorely lacking. Thirty percent are worth their weight in gold—and charge that way, too.

How do you connect with someone who's good?

You must be resourceful and do an enormous amount of homework. Get the name of every previous client, particularly *recent* clients. Grill them relentlessly. You need to know exactly what services were performed, and what results were achieved.

Once you've made your choice, enter into a *written* contract with your consultant. Make sure that you can terminate it at any time, no questions asked, with a fixed price to exit.

Now let me tell you one of my own war stories, and why I'm sold on consultants.

When I first got started in my own business I was very knowledgeable about sales and marketing. I'd spent five years selling envelopes, and I could do it in my sleep. In fact, as my wife will attest, I did do it in my sleep.

Now I wanted to make my own envelopes instead of selling someone else's. If you're in manufacturing, there are two concepts you have to master: (1) making your goods at the lowest possible price without sacrificing quality, and (2) selling them at a higher price than it costs you to make them.

Simple? Then why after three years did I find myself teetering on the edge of chapter 11? I was doing all right on number one but old number two had me on the ropes. In those three years I had gone through three factory managers, and I still couldn't knock out an envelope and sell it at a profit.

So I decided to try and find a consultant who could help me. My reasoning was this: There were 250 competing envelope companies in the country. The right cost-specialist consulting firm had probably been in at least 25 of my competitors' plants. I could take advantage of their cumulative knowledge of the industry and not have to rely on my factory manager to install a cost system dreamed up out of his own limited experience.

Machine speeds . . . output per hour . . . rejection rates . . . productive capacity . . . customer returns . . . waste. What does a guy like me, who can barely turn on a light switch, know about this stuff?

Who's likely to have the better grasp of what's needed: someone who's installed 25 systems, or someone who may never have installed any, and at best has worked with one or two?

Thirty years later, my Spencer Tucker and Associates cost system still lives at Mackay Envelope. No one-shot Band-Aid treatment here. Their system has been profitable every year since it was installed. This consulting firm has worked with over 75 envelope manufacturers and eventually became, in my opinion, the number one adviser in my industry. I'm lucky. I got in with them on the ground floor.

MACKAY'S MORAL:

Good advice is never cheap. Cheap advice is never good.

Chapter 71

LET OTHER PEOPLE MAKE YOU LOOK SMART

I'm a huge fan of creative newsletters, which I like to read to get *my* creative juices flowing. One of the best is a simple post-card called *imp*, billed as the world's smallest newsletter. Bob Westenberg, a friend who lives in Sedona, Arizona, publishes this entertaining monthly which contains about 15 to 25 aphorisms, definitions, jokes, quotes, startling facts, and more. Bob can be reached at 520-284-1111 or e-mail him at rjwesten@ sedona.net.

I've taken the liberty of sharing a few of my favorites:

Startling Facts
- Women were 1 percent of all business travelers in 1970. Today they're over 40 percent.
- Over half of retirees want to go back to work, especially after being retired for more than three months.
- Brevity is one key to clear communications. Keep it plain and simple, and get to the point. "The Gettysburg Address" contains only 268 words.
- By the time a person hits age 70, he or she will have watched seven years of TV.
- Before filing something, remember: 80 percent of everything filed is never referred to again.

- A happy customer usually tells three other people. An unhappy one tells 11.
- 28 percent of Americans go to a library at least monthly; 27 percent never go at all.
- Your risk of having a heart attack is 50 percent greater on Mondays.
- The percentage of Americans who say they trust government to do what's right has gone from over 75 percent in 1964 to under 25 percent today.
- Job interview: Schedule it in the morning. Execs found that 83 percent are more likely to hire A.M. job seekers.
- The last applicant interviewed gets the job 55.8 percent of the time. But the first interviewee is hired only 17.6 percent of the time.
- Managers spend from 25 percent to 80 percent of their time in meetings. And 53 percent of this time is unproductive.
- General Douglas MacArthur's mom accompanied him to West Point and took an apartment overlooking his dorm to be sure he studied. It worked. He graduated #1 in his class.
- Life crises can have long-term positive effects on life. Over 87 percent of people studied said crises like the death of a loved one, illness, breakup, divorce, etc., gave them a stronger sense of purpose in life.
- The average American spends 49 hours in a lifetime seeing doctors and 64 hours waiting to see them.
- The average exec wastes 30 minutes a day looking for misplaced information.
- On average, Americans open their refrigerators 22 times a day.
- In an average lifetime you'll spend four years traveling in cars and six months waiting for red lights to turn green.
- In 1975, 17 percent of Americans pumped their own gas. Today it's 78 percent.
- 56 percent of divorced Americans lived together before they were married.

- 50 percent of loans made to family members are never repaid; at least 75 percent of those made to friends are also unpaid.
- Replace bad habits with good habits. Use mental images to picture the desired end result. It takes about 21 days to form most habits, good or bad.

Business Mistakes

- Walt Disney was once fired by a newspaper. The reason? Lack of ideas.
- Memo by MGM exec after Fred Astaire's first screen test in 1933: "Can't act. Slightly bald. Can dance a little."
- Bette Davis, Clark Gable, Maurice Chevalier, Shirley Temple, and Laurence Olivier all failed their screen tests.
- Louisa May Alcott's family advised her to find work as a servant; Beethoven's violin teacher declared him hopeless as a composer.
- IBM, GE, RCA all rejected the Xerox machine. Parker Brothers turned down Trivial Pursuit. The creator of Life Savers sold the company for $2,900.

Quotes

- "I had a terrible time remembering names. Then I took the Dave Carnegie course and I've been fine ever since."
- When asked, "Does your advertising get results?" a jeweler said, "You bet! Last week we advertised for a night watchman and the next night we were robbed."

MACKAY'S MORAL:

Be a smarty-pants—tuck little ideas, frisky facts, notable quotables into your business bag of tricks.

Chapter 72

GOLDEN OLDIES

Not too many people get fired for being young. But millions get fired because they come across as over the hill. In other words: old.

Age discrimination laws may have saved many an ageless wonder, but a geezer is a geezer. You can't expect to survive, much less thrive, unless you can keep up with the rest of the pack, no matter what your age.

Chronological age in itself is no longer the "career-kiss-of-death" it once was. A recent survey by the Association of Outplacement Consulting Firms International found that workers between 50 and 70 years of age are increasingly in demand by small- and mid-sized companies. One of those companies which enthusiastically hires workers over 50 is the Dilenschneider Group, a public relations firm in Manhattan. And James Challenger, president of the executive search and outplacement firm Challenger, Gray & Christmas, notes, "We are entering an era of age neutrality."

But workers who behave old will always face discrimination. Acting "old" means being a closed system which doesn't take in new ideas. Some of us get old and some of us, despite the years, stay young. Why the difference? Part of it may be genetic. But more of this entity we call "staying young" is due to simple common sense. Youthful middle-age employees know that youthfulness is marketable. Here are some of the ways they're able to present themselves as youthful:

- They don't let themselves become "The Frightened." If the office is introducing a new networking software, they're curious about how it'll work. They're not scared that they can't learn it. If there are rumors of a layoff, they know they can do lots of other things to earn a buck. And, if necessary, they'll learn to live on less money. In the eyes of the world, scared means old.

- They recognize that kids are their number-one information resource. They pick kids' brains at home, at work, and on the commuter train. From kids they find out what new values are emerging in society. This data helps them have good relationships with their younger bosses and clients. Investment genius Warren Buffett, who's no spring chicken, likes to pal around with high-tech Seattle kid Bill Gates, who's no longer a spring chicken but still enjoys his reputation as a boy wonder.

- They "get it" that their ideas aren't sacred. Nothing dates you like going on and on about how you feel about how things have changed. Yawn. Yawn. Give the world a break and talk less about your own values, and focus more on understanding why others think differently from you.

- They rarely have regrets. Regrets are the bad cholesterol of the mind. If your mind is always on what you did wrong in 1989, you're not going to spot opportunities in 1999. Think about the 50–60-year-old chief executive officer at your company. When did he or she ever discuss what could have been, mistakes, and if onlys?

Those of us who stay young as we chronologically age have another distinct advantage in the workplace. And that's our new-found empathy. In *Getting over Getting Older*, author Letty Cottin Pogrebin points out that with age we soften emotionally and we figure out how to do better in our relationships. She's right on target. Those over 40 usually have learned how to be sensitive to others. Before the Information Age we called that "wisdom." Today we call it "empathy." It lubricates human relationships. The empathetic person becomes an effective leader and team player.

Many of us are going to live to 90-plus. And many of us want to keep working as long as our health holds out. We can do that. We have to find ourselves a small- or mid-sized company—or start our own business. We have to fight off getting too settled or too attached to our creature comforts. Executives who think they can only live in a five-bedroom house in one particular suburb are going to get old fast. And we have to make the best use of our new wisdom.

MACKAY'S MORAL:

Don't act your age, act the age you are in.

Chapter 73

CONTINUING ED

Ed was brilliant, creative, honest, and hard working, but he was one of those guys who just couldn't work with other people. Somewhere along the line there would always be a big personality conflict. Ed didn't discriminate. He could make enemies of bosses, underlings, or peers, men or women of any race, creed, or national origin.

Fortunately for Ed, he was good at what he did, and he could make a fairly decent living all by his lonesome. And he did for many years—as a freelancer, with just a handful of clients who would put up with him because of his talent, reliability, and ability to make money for them.

There are lots of Eds around. You'll find them among writers, inventors, designers, entrepreneurs, consultants, scientists, traders.

They dance to their own tune.

If you are an Ed, my message to you is that it's probably okay to be stubborn and independent in your own area of expertise—if you can get away with it. But there are certain trappings of civilization that you might want to adopt if you expect to keep yourself in the game.

First: Play by the rules—in the broadest sense of the term. If you're a boxer, that means you don't chew on your opponent's ear. For those not earning their living in the ring, that means you do not abuse your customers. Seems elementary, doesn't it? But there are people who do abuse their customers and somehow expect those customers to continue to patronize them. Long waits in line or on the telephone, bungled orders, bad attitudes, runarounds, poor responses to complaints are all abusive.

You may be the smartest stockbroker, operate the best restaurant, or be the greatest marketing genius in the land, but no matter how long the lines are in front of your shop today, the nanosecond you slip or your competition even begins to approach your performance, your customers will vanish.

Not everyone can be number one in performance. How do the number twos and threes and fours and fives and tens survive in competitive industries? By the way they treat their customers. Performance may vary from one period or product cycle to the next, but if courtesy, concern, caring, and consideration remain at a high level, customers will tend to remain loyal.

Second: Don't neglect the little things. If you're an Ed, one of the reasons you left the rat race was so that no one could tell you how to run your business. So what if you're still using a one-line phone system to carry your fax, your business calls, your personal calls, and your Internet, and your customers are complaining your line is always busy? So what if you haven't shined your shoes since you bought them? As long as you perform, who cares? Well, your customers do care. Businesses buff up because they know that outdated technology and shabby appearances convey an impression, whether true or not, of tired ideas.

Third: Much as you'd like to, you really can't go it alone. You have to keep up. If the last time you darkened the door of an educational institution was to attend a reunion, you are slipping beneath the waves whether you know it or not. Much as the Eds of the world hate "fluff" like seminars, training sessions, workshops, professional magazines, classes, and conventions, you have to get with the program. Certain professionals, like doctors, lawyers, and accountants, are legally required to take anywhere from 10 to 25 hours per year of continuing education just to keep their licenses.

The rest of us may not be violating the law of the state by failing to hone our skills, but we will quickly discover we are on the short end of the law of the jungle: survival of the fittest.

As for Ed, before all his business drifts away, he might try Dale Carnegie or Toastmasters and see if they can uncover some hidden charm.

MACKAY'S MORAL:

Doing things in the good old ways they were done in the good old days is just that. Old.

Section Five

GOING FIRST CLASS

HANDLE WITH CARE

Chapter 74

THERE IS A LIMITED MARKET FOR ONE-TRICK PONIES

Last year I was asked at the last minute to substitute for another speaker. It didn't take any great insight on my part to figure out I was probably not the first person who had been approached, since the scheduled speaker was the vice president of the United States, Al Gore, who was needed back in Washington. The group I was asked to speak to was the National Bar Association, the organization of African American lawyers and judges.

I accepted.

It didn't go too badly. I even got a little laugh on my opener: "Well, you didn't get the vice president, but you did get the president . . . of Mackay Envelope Corporation."

From time to time, we all have been asked to pinch hit or to take on jobs we may not have been expecting or been fully prepared to perform.

My sermon on this topic is: Do it anyway.

No, not for the learning experience. Do it because there is no surer way I know of to get ahead than to take on a high-pressure assignment on short notice with limited firepower.

Jack Welch of General Electric has supercharged versatility into a management concept he calls "boundarylessness." Welch is obsessed with banishing the "not invented here" syndrome that dooms ideas to certain death when they are conceived in one department and handed over to another. To Jack Welch the best idea is the best idea, no matter where it comes from or who thought of it, and to facilitate that, he has broken down the walls in the traditional corporate structure: He tackles problems with interdepartmental teams.

Anyone who owns General Electric stock knows how successful that seemingly simple idea has been. Yet very few companies practice it.

The advertising business is driven by creativity and crippled by compartmentalization. There is no law that says only art directors can have great visual concepts and only copy writers can have great verbal concepts. There is no law that says all art directors have to sit in one corner of the office and copy writers must be huddled by themselves in another.

Fallon McElligott, one of the country's perennially hottest advertising shops, is so committed to cross-pollination, that the desks and art directors' boards are on wheels.

Where people can flow, ideas flow.

If you want to make your own juices flow a little more freely, let me suggest this: Learn a new skill or find a new outlet for your talents. It doesn't much matter what it is, a second language, public speaking, volunteer work. It will help you overcome your fear of flying. The next time the boss says, "I need someone who'll . . . fill in for Larry for a couple of weeks/open a new territory/tackle this problem," you just might be a little more willing to rise to the challenge. After all, you've already proven to yourself you can do it.

Don't worry, most of the time they'll cut you some slack. When my call came, no one expected me to top the veep, and I didn't, but I still got an A for effort.

And so will you.

MACKAY'S MORAL

Roll with the punches, go with the flow,
ride your pony, and don't yell whooooooaa!

Chapter 75

ACTING SMART AND BEING SMART

Of all the human failings that can destroy a business, arrogance is the deadliest. It is the most readily acquired, the easiest to justify, and the hardest to recognize in ourselves.

It's different from greed, laziness, or dishonesty. These faults are usually individual flaws, not contagious to entire companies. We know them when we see them, and we know they are wrong. When they are detected, correction is usually swift, certain, and severe.

But arrogance?

When we're successful, we reason, don't we deserve a bit of special consideration? Aren't we important enough to avoid the everyday annoyances and the tedious responsibilities that ordinary mortals must endure? No one is "entitled" to be dishonest or greedy, but a bit of smugness, well, that's just natural in a leader. We accept it. We even nurture it as a sign of success.

But arrogance can infect all the employees in a company with the silent destructiveness of a computer virus. After all, if the company is making money big-time, and everyone in the shop has a chip on their shoulder, then shoulder chips are right, proper, and normal, aren't they? It's like the few, the proud, the marines. Okay for landing on contested beaches, but dangerous when carved into the brain pans of, say, envelope makers.

I found it interesting to read about the difference in style between John Akers, the deposed head of IBM, and his successor, Louis Gerstner. "Unlike Akers, who used to enter and leave the building via a rear elevator and was rarely seen around the headquarters offices, Gerstner began walking around, sticking his head into people's offices to ask how they were progressing on some assignment he'd given them," according to *Big Blues: The Unmaking of IBM*, by Paul Carroll, a newly published history of the company that was once the showcase of American management.

The disease that felled IBM wasn't technological incompetence. It was arrogance. The people at the top had lost their ability to communicate. They were unwilling to work the trenches. That was for the grunts. Executives don't have to bother with that sort of thing. They had their own elevator. Why listen to the marketplace? They *were* the marketplace.

Joe Batten's *Tough-Minded Leadership* includes a kind of ten commandments of management. The basic principles are set out in the form of a pledge, which managers make to the people they supervise. Here's one that grabbed me:

> I promise to the members of my team:
> To show them I can *do* as well as manage by pitching in
> to work beside them when my help is needed.

The higher up you go, the more important it is for you to stay in touch, both with your customers and your employees. You don't have to put your hand in a grain roller to prove you're a *mensch*, but you should walk your plant every day. Don Burr, founder and CEO of the now-defunct Peoples Express airline, went from zero to billions in sales virtually overnight. His meteoric rise plopped him on the cover of *Time* magazine. He once told me that among the many mistakes causing their collapse, arrogance led the list.

How do you know when you're getting arrogant? When the only people you care to listen to or deal with are either at your own level or above it.

MACKAY'S MORAL

Arrogance is believing you're so high up that you don't have to keep an ear to the ground.

Chapter 76

THE FUTURE ISN'T JUST AROUND THE CORNER, IT'S RIGHT ACROSS THE DESK

At a speech not long ago, Bill Gates was asked: "If you were graduating from college right now, would you go to work for Microsoft or start your own company?"

His answer, which brought down the house, was, "Well I wouldn't know. I never graduated from college." The most famous Harvard dropout in history went on to emphasize how incredibly important it is for companies to make work "as fun and interesting" for new employees as possible.

Given all the productivity-oriented pep talks I've heard about leadership, it was surprising to hear someone highlighting "fun and interesting" as managerial objectives. I can count on one finger the times I've strolled through the envelope plant to see whether people were having fun. But it raises an interesting issue about the changing nature of today's workforce.

An executive friend recently laid it on the line for his employees in the formal conference room of his venerable East Coast consulting firm. If office profitability didn't improve drastically, individual bonuses would be severely affected. Worse, their office would lose status within the corporation.

In response, the old guard dutifully put their shoulders to the wheel and gave a renewed heave. However, the younger set appeared nonplused, demonstrating a distinct lack of shame for their failure to bear the company banner with the expected degree of pride. In truth, they seemed resentful.

And their complaints started drifting, actually slamming, their way into the executive offices—complaints about loss of free time, being watched by "big brother," working in a depressing place, and too much dues-paying. Far from being moved by the boss's proclamations on loyalty and duty, the talented twenty-somethings had labeled him a *drag*.

At a loss, he called a face-to-face meeting. What he heard was the opening volley in a revolution.

"You keep talking about bonuses," they told him. "But if it's no fun to work here, and if we're not learning, bonuses don't mean much.

"And another thing. You always talk about loyalty, but you're never around. We want managers we can connect with."

My friend had just been served a summons. And if he didn't respond, he'd be tried and convicted before he even knew what happened. Not convicted by a jury of peers who speak his language and play by his rules. This jury is younger, more mobile, more disenfranchised, more skeptical, more vocal, and much, much less impressed with the boss's values and achievements than any generation that's gone before.

Marketers have a name for them, of course. They're "Generation Xers." They are the generation of 46 million people who are the children of the Baby Boomers, born after WW II, who have now grown up. We didn't hear a lot from them while they were in grade school, but they're in the workforce now and influential enough to make considerable noise.

But management has been slow to figure out that its employee base is changing. Those of us who were relieved to see our Generation X kids leave the nest are shocked to find them sitting across the desk from us. And everything we didn't learn about managing them before is back to haunt us now.

What do we need to know about them? When asked in a recent survey to rank the 10 most significant attributes they looked for in a job, younger workers ranked compensation seventh out of 10! More significant to them were recognition and praise, opportunities to learn, time spent with mentors, developing marketable skills, and fun at work.

What turns them off? Consultant Lynne Lancaster is a partner in the Minneapolis-based company Bridge Works, which specializes in bridging the generation gap. She says Gen Xers don't like hearing about the past, especially *ours*. "They also resent inflexibility in scheduling, being micromanaged, feeling pressured to conform, and being viewed as lazy or unambitious. In other words, a lot of the standard carrot-and-stick approaches to management that worked for the Baby Boomers are a bust with this crowd."

What can we do about it?

"Question the way you manage and reward people," says Lancaster. "This is a group that very much wants to succeed. Ask them questions. Listen. Rethink your concept of motivation. Not everyone in the workplace is motivated by the same thing anymore. To get the most out of this talented new workforce, you have to be willing to change, to become more flexible. For managers and companies that learn to do this, it will be incredibly rewarding."

Maybe even—heaven forbid—fun!

MACKAY'S MORAL

If you're looking across the desk and seeing your own image, you might just be hallucinating.

Chapter 77

Unconventional Wisdom

Warren Bennis's title is "University Professor and Distinguished Professor of Business Administration" at the University of Southern California. He serves on a number of high-powered boards. He has written several popular, readable, and practical business books. I got to know him well when I sat on his board of directors for the Leadership Institute in the Graduate School of Business at USC.

Warren Bennis understands and keeps pace with modern business practices. He does not do anything by accident.

I received a thank-you note from him a while ago. The note was hand-written. The envelope was hand-addressed.

If I could choose to give one, small, inexpensive gift to everyone who reads this book on the basis of what would make the most positive impact on their lives, it would be an easy call: No, it wouldn't be one of my books. It would be a fountain pen.

The more PCs they sell, the more valuable those fountain pens get.

Look through your mail. Every scrap of paper in the heap is either printed or word processed, isn't it? You're lucky if your kids sign your birthday cards. A hand-written note in real ink on real stationery stands out a bit, doesn't it?

It says the writer cares.

It says you are special.

It says it in a way no computer-crunched message can.

The real pros have known that for a long time. Though

we've gotten used to thinking of politics as totally media driven, it isn't. Politicians would love to be able to win elections just by spouting 20-second sound bites. But it's just not that easy. Politics is a retail business as much as it is a wholesale one. You have to sell one customer at a time. It's like football. The game is won in the trenches, not with 40-yard passes. Successful pols like George Bush and Bill Clinton have spent a lifetime doing the blocking and tackling, the hard fundamentals of the trade, by hand-writing short notes. Everyone to whom they can conceivably claim a connection or bestow a pat on the back gets one. Shook the Big Guy's hand at a potluck supper? Won a bowling tournament? Endured 50 years of marital bliss? You're on the daily list.

The more technologically festooned our lives become, the more important the personal touch becomes.

It isn't even necessary to use the ultimate weapon, the fountain pen. A regular pen will do.

Taking care of your customers means more than price, product, and delivery. It means showing you care about them. As individual, living, breathing human beings.

MACKAY'S MORAL

Only a computer wants to do business with another computer. People respond to people.

Chapter 78

THE BEST WAY TO GET EVEN IS TO FORGIVE

In Victor Hugo's epic, and the Broadway play, *Les Misérables*, the newly paroled Jean Valjean, unable to find work, starving, comes upon a priest who shelters and feeds him. At dinner he eyes the silver candlesticks on the table while he is wolfing down the food, later steals them, flees, only to be stopped on a routine check of "papers" by the gendarmes. When the police haul him back to the abbey to confirm that the goods are stolen, the priest, incredibly, tells the authorities that the candlesticks were a "gift" to Valjean, thereby sparing him a renewed sentence of life at hard labor. Valjean, empowered by the priest's daring forgiveness, achieves significant social status and gets a second chance at life.

Our lives are full of random blows to the sternum that have left us breathless, enraged, and sometimes bitter. Some are very impersonal, disheartening—credit card theft, a car that has been "keyed," or recently, a stolen putter. I can't forgive the weasels because I don't know who they are, for crying out loud! Just a bunch of losers, I guess.

Other barrages are highly personal. Cheating spouses, drunk drivers, unjust wars, abduction, rape, incest—black holes of personal terror that I hope none of us ever experience. God bless those that have crossed bridges to forgiveness. From my perspective, it seems almost impossible.

But, what about the hits—the clips you take on an every-month basis? In sports, do you remember the jersey number as you fall so that you can hit 'em later when they're least suspecting? The person who end-runs you to your boss, or takes leadership credit for the work you did—this is the stuff of normal business life. How about the disparaging remarks at the cocktail party that get back to you about what kind of boss you really are? Or the joker who confronts you with the embarrassing question of "How much do you make?" at the company meeting?

The answer? Forgive them. In the vast scheme of things, the personal slights mean nothing, and your stature will only be enhanced if you are able to take the high road. This isn't to say that you play "dead bug," a strategy that places your feet and arms straight up in the air while you are hoping not to get stepped on. Acknowledge, address, or confront the affront, but before the pot boils over in the conversation, tell him or her that you forgive them—and mean it. The next look on their face will be priceless, I guarantee it.

But how about if it's a more damaging blow? One that definitely sets you back in your career, hits your wallet significantly, or affects a loved one. A false rumor about you or your past, a stolen idea, a key employee wooed by a friend, a secretary or trusted associate who betrays a very, very private confidence—all rank up there with the worst of them. It's a tough call not to declare World War III at that point, and much may depend upon whether the perpetrator is conciliatory and/or apologetic. But after a good night's sleep, I'll usually side with "every dog gets one bite."

My reasoning is simple and self-reflective. Everybody, and I mean everybody, screws up, hurts others, finds fault, misjudges, and acts emotionally and improperly from time to time at the expense of others. Recognizing this, I'll forgive the padded expense account the first time, the vendor who blunders over prices, and the exaggerated time card. And I know my character will strengthen when I have to work hard to forgive the deal makers who tried to cut me out of the deal, the bankers who wouldn't lend me money when tough times rolled to town, the sales rep who left me for a "sweeter" deal and returned.

And if the day is done, and I can't forgive them, I forget them.

So here, just as well as anywhere, I better take my own medicine. I forgive you Jim, Liz, and Tom.

MACKAY'S MORAL

Every dog gets one bite.

Chapter 79

GET IN THE SWING OF PRACTICING

Dan Jenkins, the author of a number of popular sports novels, including *Semi-Tough* and *Dead Solid Perfect*, once wrote that no one could ever actually see a goal scored in hockey.

That's the reason that hockey has the lowest TV ratings of all the major sports. Tennis, too, has recently had problems in attracting a national viewing audience. With 125-mile-per-hour serves in the men's game, you rarely see a tennis ball hit more than a few times per point, and the five-set marathons make it tough to hold spectators. It also kills TV programming because the networks never know when the match is going to end.

Tennis is losing its grip, and not just on the tube. Every sport needs heroes. Golf has a Tiger on the tee, but presently there aren't any young American tennis players with Tiger Woods's charisma. My tennis cronies are leaving the game in droves and opting for golf. So far, I love both sports equally.

Golf for business purposes is exploding through the sound barrier. Twenty million rounds of business golf will be played this year.

Why?

TV and Tiger are factors, but there's another that hasn't gotten much notice, and that's the change in the makeup of the American workforce.

Golf is a networking game par excellence. In what other environment can you see your customer for four hours straight?

Women are taking giant leaps in business, where we good old boys have had it pretty much to ourselves. And women in droves are also taking up golf, another area where we good old boys once reigned supreme.

Until recent years, women weren't allowed on most private courses during prime time: Wednesday and Saturday and Sunday mornings. They are now, and they're turning out in record numbers with a determination to excel.

Here are a few tips I learned from a woman I described in my last book as a "former junior golf champ with a closet full of trophies." Her name then was Carol Ann Miller, but for the last 38 years she's been Carol Ann Mackay.

1. Ask the best player you know for the name of his or her instructor. Try another one or two. Pick the one you're most comfortable with. Don't skip from one instructor to another looking for a quick fix.

2. Insist on a video of your swing. Watch the video. Frequently. Do not ever erase that video. Keep making and watching new videos. The object is to improve.

3. Always place a tape recorder next to the practice balls and record your lesson. It's the moral equivalent of taking notes in a class, only it's easier.

4. After your lesson, don't start your car until you have actually jotted down everything you can remember in your own words. We forget 50 percent of what we hear in four hours—and that's on good days.

5. Make an investment and take a playing lesson with the pro. This is not a violation of rule #1. It's part of the 10-point plan.

6. Have your teacher give you the titles of the six best golf books that have ever been written. Three for the physical game and three for the mental stuff.

7. Hang out and play with good golfers. It will soak in. (Aristotle, who didn't play golf, had a variant of this advice in describing how to improve oneself as a human being. In the words of the Greek philosopher, "Hang with good people.")

8. Watch golf on TV.

9. Watch the pros play when they come to town.

10. Enter club tournaments (A, B, C class) so your nervousness will eventually go away.

Thanks, Carol Ann, but you left something out:

MACKAY'S MORAL

11. Beat your customer at your own risk.

Chapter 80

STILL BUTTONED UP?

My father needed a suit. He went to a store, where a salesman introduced himself and asked my father his name. "Jack Mackay? Aren't you *Doctor* Mackay?" For the next 40 years my father bought suits from this guy, who played this stunt so often, his nickname was, of course, "Doc."

In those days, white-collar workers actually were white-collar workers. Their suits were their uniforms. Every salesperson of a certain age can remember being told that if you expect to be taken seriously by a CEO, you better look like one.

And so we did, or at least like our sales managers' fantasies of how a CEO was supposed to look. Suit, tie, white shirt—no short sleeves, either.

It didn't matter that no one, not even a bank president, dressed that way in smaller towns. We did. Until the technological revolution.

Technological change isn't just about technology. Take a look at Bill Gates and all the Bill Gates wannabes. See any suits and ties?

Call on a CEO today, and he or she may be 26 years old, wear jeans and a Grateful Dead T-shirt, and pull up next to you in the parking lot on a bicycle. And still have a net worth greater than the GNP of Guatemala.

Thanks to technology, the Silicon Valley dress code is now de rigueur from coast-to-coast.

A while ago IBM announced that they were abandoning their traditional dress code in favor of the more casual approach. IBM was the last of the big-time holdouts. For the last 10 years or so, whenever you saw someone under 60 in a white shirt, suit, and tie, you could be sure they were with either IBM or the FBI.

Why did IBM finally cave? It was not to make the employees feel more comfortable. Lou Gerstner, who came from R.J. Reynolds before he took over as head of IBM, is the ultimate marketing man. A company that's supposed to be on the cutting edge of technological change shouldn't require their employees to dress like clones from *The Man in the Gray Flannel Suit*.

Easy for IBM to take the great leap forward, but not for clothing manufacturers and retailers. They're selling a hell of a lot fewer suits, and no matter how hard they try to glamorize the new look, there's no way they can get $400 or so for the kind of outfits their customers are used to wearing to take out the garbage. It's not just dress codes that are vanishing because of technology.

Remember "office hours"? Woody Allen said, "Eighty percent of life is just showing up." The phone company—when there was only one company that answered to that description—proved it. They used to require their salespeople to be at their desks at 8 A.M. and be back there at 5 P.M. How they performed in between didn't much matter. Even after the breakup of the company, it took a long time for the culture to change.

Competitors knew that phone company salespeople had to get their cars back to the motor pool by 4:30 P.M., so they made their appointments for 5 P.M., took the customers out for a drink, beat the phone company's deal, and signed them up.

Today, the numbers the phone company cares about are not on the clock but in the sales quotas. Salespeople can spend their working lives any way they care to, just so long as they hit their sales marks.

More victims of technological change: As the old rules have vanished so have the people who have been enforcing them. The middle managers, the guardians of the corporate culture, who checked out your wing tips and made sure you were at your desk on time, aren't needed anymore. The rules they enforced don't contribute to the bottom line. And corporate cultures don't mean much in an environment where the employee or even the corporation itself may disappear tomorrow.

MACKAY'S MORAL

The new "dress for success" is a lot more
concerned with success than dress.

Don't Wait
for Publishers'
Sweepstakes

Chapter 81

PEOPLE DON'T PLAN TO FAIL, THEY FAIL TO PLAN

Just a gentle reminder to all the stock market geniuses out there: Making money is not always quite as easy as it seems.

Ginger is a happy, healthy, attractive, well-to-do, married woman who lives in a lovely lakeside home in a Minneapolis suburb. She has a good life. Not much rattles her.

Just don't mention "root beer" around Ginger.

In the early '50s, when Ginger was a teenager, her dad decided to make his fortune in the root beer game. One of Ginger's dad's relatives was in the construction business in Iowa. He had built a number of root beer stands for clients, seen them prosper, and convinced Ginger's dad to move the entire family down to Iowa for the summer and open his own stand.

"It costs less than two cents for the root beer. You sell it for a dime. That's a 500 percent markup. With the whole family pitching in, it's a license to steal. How can you lose?"

Stay tuned.

Problem #1. Location.

The stand was on the highway between Arnold's Park, a popular amusement park, and Lake Okoboji. (If you know Iowa, then you know that's about the only lake in the state.) Sounds good, but unfortunately, while the general location was excellent, they picked a miserable site. Ginger's relative knew a lot about the construction business, but he didn't know anything about the fast-food business. He had built the stand so that it wasn't visible to motorists until they had already practically driven past it. These days, any food chain worth its buns has location experts who help design the site to maximize its potential.

Problem #2. Doing business with relatives.

Dad's dear old relative had promised to have the stand ready in time for Memorial Day, the first big selling day of the year. He didn't. The fact that he was a relative made it tough for dad to get tough. Instead of spending Memorial Day selling root beer, the family spent that weekend painting the stand as cars whizzed by.

Problem #3. Lack of contingency planning.

The second big selling day of the year was the Fourth of July. At about 10 A.M. the compressor that ran the root beer dispenser froze up. Ginger's family didn't really know anybody in Iowa, so there was no one they could call for emergency repairs. They made history though. They were the only root beer stand in America that didn't sell any root beer that day.

Problem #4. Flawed marketing plans.

One day in August they decided to jack up food sales by having the family pass out coupons for free root beer to passersby on the road. It turned out to be their top root beer day of the year . . . free root beer, that is. Food sales were nonexistent. On second thought, they shouldn't have done their promotion right after lunch when everyone was full and only thirsty. They ran out of root beer. Angry people trashed the area with crumpled-up coupons.

Problem #5. The gods were angry, too.

Labor Day was the last big day of the season. They were

determined to make up for everything that had gone wrong. They ordered enough food and root beer to feed the entire population of Iowa. Ginger's dad paid top dollar to get the highest-quality hamburgers and hot dogs.

Everyone was on board but the weather man. They had torrential rain all morning and business was so bad they shut down by noon.

Ginger rode back home to Minneapolis later that week in the back of her dad's car with her sisters. They were juggling about 100 pounds of high-grade hamburger on their laps that was starting to go bad. Just to put a fitting cap on the summer, the car broke down about 60 miles from home.

MACKAY'S MORAL

Ever heard of Callahan's Corollary? It says Murphy was an optimist.

R.S.V.P.
REWARDS. SERVICE.
VALUE. PRICE.

Chapter 82

TAKE A TIP
FROM HARVEY

One of the little secrets of the managerial game is to reward productive employees with bonuses rather than salary increases.

A bonus is used to recognize measurable past performance, both by the employee and the company itself. When company results and individual performance are both good, bonuses go up. When they're not so good, bonuses go down.

When the employee does poorly but the company has a good year, most employers will base their bonuses on individual performance.

The tough call comes when the employee does well, but the company doesn't. On Wall Street the employees walk home with the loot, while the shareholders suffer. Even Warren Buffett, who was a principal owner of Salomon Brothers at one time, wasn't able to change that culture, but let me assure you, it's not done that way in any other business that I'm familiar with. The employer who uses the bonus has an excuse to resolve the split decision in the company's own favor.

Baseball provides the classic story on this theme.

Before free agency, there were no long-term contracts. Players' salaries were more like bonuses: one-year contracts were tied to the previous year's performance.

Ned Garver, who won an amazing 20 games for the perennial cellar-dwelling St. Louis Browns, asked his boss, Bill Veeck, for a raise on next year's salary.

"No," Veeck told Garver. "We could have finished last without you."

If you'll pardon a bad rhyme:

> There's no onus
> To lowering a bonus;
> But when it's a raise,
> It's forever and always.

Tipping is a kind of bonus. Employers love to have their employees dependent on tips for a major portion of their income. It enables them to pay penurious salaries, and puts the responsibility of taking up the slack on the customer. If the tip is lousy, who does the tippee blame? Not his cheap employer, but the cheap customer.

Let me be honest about this: Sometimes I'm that cheap customer. When I go to a restaurant, if I'm treated rudely or get pathetic service, I make sure I knock that tip down accordingly. It's not just being tough, it's tough love. If I'm going to provide someone with a slice of their income, then the slice I provide depends on the quality of the service I get. When I send a strong signal to that effect, the recipient quickly learns that what they get depends on what they deliver.

Here's another piece of my upside-down, bubble-gum psychology. If I'm at a resort, my experience usually centers around the tennis court. I'm at the mercy of the tennis pro to fix me up with a variety of games at my level, or above, and to give me lessons and pointers. Will the vacation be an ace or a whiff? It depends almost entirely on how well it goes for me with the pro.

I do not wait and tip at the end of the week. No. I may be at the pro's mercy, but I'm not going to put him at mine. I meet with him on day one, tell him what I would like to accomplish, how long I'll be there, and most importantly, thank him in advance with a generous tip.

I've never agreed with the philosophy that you sweat the pro for a week and keep him guessing as to whether or not you're a good tipper.

Why is the resort different from the restaurant? At the resort, you're there for the duration, not an hour and a half. No one can afford to be miserable that long. Give the people you need the benefit of the doubt, take care of them appropriately and immediately, and they will respond with first-cabin service.

MACKAY'S MORAL

Use tips the way an employer uses bonuses:
to reward and ensure performance, not to perform
a meaningless social ritual.

Chapter 83

THE PRICE IS RIGHT . . . BUT FOR WHOM?

Money is a subject we take very, very seriously. What's surprising is how weird we are about how we spend it. Every one of us, rich or poor, has some spending habit that can only be described as irrational.

I'm an addicted jogger. It's a day wasted if I don't do IT. But I'll turn in my Nikes before I'll walk an extra 20 feet to get to my car at a stadium parking lot. Five bucks more for a preferred parking spot? Sure. Valet parking? A tenner plus a tip? You bet. I tell myself I'm buying getaway time, but I'm not. The parking spaces closest to the gate are usually the ones that provide the quickest access to the road, and if I can make four miles, I should be able to make it to any gate in the country. What I'm really doing is extending my willingness to buy a front-row seat for the game into buying a front-row seat for my car. It's dumb, but it's an almost universal kind of dumbness. People park their cars to match their seats.

Many retailers make a nice living from this kind of twisted logic.

In our not-so-classless society, price will always be a major differentiator. Price, not quality. Sometimes the less difference in quality there is, the more difference in price. Why? You have to find some way to differentiate your product or service. There are always going to be people willing to pay more just to set themselves apart from people who won't.

Most of us like to think we're immune to this kind of price snobbery. Are we?

Look at your wrist. What kind of watch are you wearing? A $20 quartz watch will tell time just as well as a $5,000 mechanical watch, but displays of affluence, not accuracy, are the basis for a very large segment of the watch market.

Do you save your frequent flier miles, yearning for an upgrade that can separate you from the thundering herd? The front of the plane doesn't arrive any sooner than the back. Some first-class fliers are seated up front so they can be duly recognized as such by the passengers passing through on their way to the cheap seats in the back.

According to Mercer Management Consulting's Jacques Cesar and Matthew Isotta, although most people will claim that price is a prime motivator in their buying decisions, their behavior often suggests otherwise.

"In many situations, only 15 to 30 percent of customers are *truly* price sensitive," Cesar and Isotta say. The rest of us are too lazy to react to price changes. The Mercer people think many retailers fail to understand this and as a result, they provide discounts to all their customers instead of just those who are really price motivated. Discounts should be targeted to the people who won't shop without them, not to the 70 to 85 percent of us who will.

Mercer gives an example. Hotels like advance bookings, as far in the future as possible. It gives them pricing power because they can project capacity. It saves them money by increasing flexibility in ordering food, beverages, supplies, and arranging work schedules. Market research shows that most hotel customers don't want to book more than two weeks in advance. In order to attract guests who are price conscious without shaving prices for customers who aren't, Mercer suggests that hotels provide a special discount to those who are willing to book at least three weeks in advance.

The same principle applies to any business. Smart retailers adjust prices for customers willing to do business on terms advantageous to the retailer. What's advantageous? It changes every day. It could be a willingness to buy in volume. Agree to immediate or delayed delivery. Accept poorer—or better—quality, or a different color, style, season, or fashion than originally specified. Accelerate payment. There are countless variables.

Most of us are willing to give a little on one or two of them, but there's always a point at which we draw the line. I'm always looking to save a buck the same as anyone else. I'm agreeable to paying up front to get a concession on price, and I'm usually not fussy about delivery. But hey, I won't take it in fuchsia even if you give it to me.

Whether it's parking or pinstripes, smart retailers are constantly tweaking these little irrationalities in all of us to generate sales that wouldn't happen otherwise.

MACKAY'S MORAL

When someone says, "It ain't the money but the principle of the thing". . . it's the money.

Chapter 84

. . . And Miles to Go Before I Sleep

Until we figure out a way to fax ourselves across the country, business travel will remain an inescapable part of modern life. We all have our little tricks to make it less painful. Here are some of mine:

Packing
- **Less is more.** A max of two of everything, one on your back and one in the bag, except shirts, ties, socks, and underwear. Use the hotel laundry. Not cheap, but fast and efficient. Don't bother with shampoo, unless you like to brush your teeth with the stuff since the bottles always leak all over the bottom of your toilet kit. Besides, almost every place furnishes it. Also, keep your toothbrush in one of those little plastic sleeves or you'll always get gunk of some kind on it.
- **My briefcase.** A miniature life-support system. Partial list of contents: emergency Snickers bar for those magic moments when the plane is four hours late and out of food; cellular phone; minidictating machine; Swiss army knife; a stack of dollar bills, Post-it notes; postage stamps; envelopes.

Planes
- **Lag time.** I have both an in-flight and on-land strategy to cope with this. When I'm on the plane, I work. There is

just no way I have ever been able to sleep on an airplane. And how can you read for pleasure when you are trapped for hours in a leg immobilizer originally designed for the Spanish Inquisition and cleverly updated for modern use? The chapter you are reading here is the laptop version of two hours and 20 minutes of human suffering. For relaxing, I bring my own Walkman and blackout shades. I also drink a ton of water. It improves circulation and digestion, and overcomes the accelerated dehydration caused by travel. Once I get off the plane, I exercise as soon as I can. I run. I swim. Anything to work the kinks out.

- **Food.** Want to avoid the usual G.I. rations? You can if you order ahead of time, which is what I usually do when I make my reservations. All the domestic airlines have special menus, i.e., vegetarian, seafood, low-carb, high-protein, low-calorie. You can even order kosher. It still isn't exactly haute cuisine, but it's better than the standard issue, and they don't care whether your name's Goldberg or O'Shaughnessy.

- **Seats.** Bulkhead, because you don't have to spend the trip with the head of the person in front of you in your lap. The aisle seats in the emergency-exit row are even better, because the seats ahead of you do not recline and there's usually a few inches more leg room besides. Also, they don't seat kids in this row.

   I try to catch the sunrises and sunsets, too, by traveling portside when I'm heading south in the morning or north in the evening, starboard when it's the other way around. While the other side of the cabin is plunged into darkness, I get to eyeball the most spectacular dazzlers Mother Nature has to offer. The word "posh" has its roots in that strategy. When the English sailed to India in the glory days of the British Empire, the choicest accommodations were "port out, starboard home."

   Here's how you get the seats you want when the airline

says they don't have them. Ask this question: "Do you have any 'nonrev' passengers in those seats?" Nonrevs are nonrevenue payers, usually airplane employees or their families traveling gratis. The airline will move them for you, but only if you know how to ask.

- **Making connections.** Airlines won't schedule you to connect with a flight due to leave before your scheduled arrival, or even a few minutes after. So do it their way. But before you take the trip, make a list of the connecting flights that depart about the time your plane is supposed to get in. As soon as you get off the plane, grab the first person you see in an airline uniform and find out if any of those flights are still loading passengers. Since planes have been known to depart late, you have a decent chance of making one of these connections and saving yourself some downtime. Obviously, carry-on baggage is a must for this to work.

- **International.** Always carry a photocopy of your passport with you in a separate place. I've never lost my passport, but if I ever did, this tiny gimmick makes replacing it a lot easier.

- **Getting to the hotel.** If you're arriving at night, arrange to be picked up by a town car. It's not a limo, but it has a distinct advantage over a cab. You can get some work done. Town cars have a reading light. Cabs don't. If you're coming into New York City from LaGuardia, the town car will cost you about $10 more than it will take to get a cab to your hotel. If you figure your time is worth more than $10, the town car is the better deal.

Hotel

- **Home, sweet home.** I'm on the road so much, I not only stay at the same hotels every time I return to a city, I ask for the same room. When I'm in familiar circumstances, I'm more comfortable and at ease. I sleep better and I

> Some car rental companies will deliver a car to your hotel at no extra charge, so see if you can have a limousine service take you to your hotel and get your rental car there. You don't have to worry about reading maps late at night or getting lost on dark roads.
>
> You'll get a good night's sleep, and your car will be waiting for you when you wake up in the morning.
>
> —Robin Leach, Host of *Lifestyles of the Rich and Famous* (from *Men's Health* magazine)

work better. I don't want to get lost looking for the rest room when I'm trying to concentrate on business.

- **A hotel with a view.** I like to be located near a park because I run. And, as long as I'm going to be staying near a park, I like a room with a view. Ask. It often doesn't cost any more than a room by the elevator shaft, which in addition to being viewless, is the noisiest area in the hotel.
- **Meals.** If the person you're coming to town to meet is worth doing business with, they probably know the good places to eat. When you're arranging your meetings, ask. And take their advice. Particularly if you don't know the person. It's a good way to show confidence in them at minimum risk, and an icebreaker when you meet.

Happy trails.

> If you're in a new city and want to find a great restaurant, call the food editor of the local newspaper.
>
> —Bernard Shaw, CNN News (from *Men's Health* magazine)

MACKAY'S MORAL

Whoever said "Getting there is half the fun" did not have a lot of fun in life.

Chapter 85

No One Gets It: Good Service Sells

Dear Corporate President:

Sincerely,
Harvey Mackay

P.S. If there's one thing I'm totally sure of in life, it's that no one ever reads the letter first. They always skip right to the P.S.

Why do we do that?

Maybe it's because we've learned that's where the beef is. Four pages of "a new commitment to excellence," said 47 different ways, just doesn't hold your attention like "By the way, we've assigned your account to my brother-in-law. He's really turned the corner since his parole."

We hear talk about service. Not much about performance. I've always liked a saying in the ad game that sums it up: "Creative gets the business: account service loses it."

That's an old, old saying. But we still don't get it.

Every second of every minute of every day of ... well, you get the idea ... we run into sloppy, pathetic, irritating service. When you live at 30,000 feet and travel 100-plus days of the year as I've been doing lately, I suppose you notice it more.

- A travel agent forgets to tell the Traveling Man he must switch airports in Paris, pick up his luggage, and hoof it from one airport to the next, enroute to Spain. Result: lost luggage, lost connection.

- The Traveling Man finally arrives at his hotel, a five-star job no less, late at night. The hotel clerk is courteous and friendly. The computer is not. It spits out the following message: "We have you arriving same time tomorrow night. We're totally booked tonight. Sorry, Mr. Mackay. Have a good day. Come back and see us again real soon."

- Next stop, another five-star beauty. At last, room at the inn. But this one misspells the Traveling Man's last name, so that when an urgent call comes in, the caller is told no one by that name is registered.

- Ah, finally, stateside bound, where the Traveling Man's can-do fellow Americans are just waiting to show their stuff. First stop, a little side trip to Los Angeles, where the daughter of a close friend is being married. The scheduling is tight, but hey, the Traveling Man has got this thing licked: a town car to meet him at the airport and get him to the church on time. Result: the driver goes north and the wedding is south. The TM doesn't even get a chance to hear the vows, let alone kiss the bride.

- Home, sweet home! After the hassle and eventual return of the inevitable lost luggage, time for a little R and R while the Traveling Man gets his traveling clothes in shape for his next adventure. Victory at last! At least two-thirds of the shirts that are returned to him by the cleaners are his own!

Notice that the excursion we're talking about here is not exactly the Willy Loman special. The TM is not trying to make his program work by staying with the good folks at Motel Cheapo. Doesn't matter. Five stars. No stars. The only difference is the size of the gumdrop on the pillow.

Is there more? Of course there's more. I could have stayed home and talked with voice mail. Or listened to Sibelius or "Achy Breaky Heart" while I was waiting to talk with voice mail. I could have had my car fixed. Or rather, returned unfixed. I could have done lots of good stuff like that there, but it would have all turned out the same.

No service.

Yes, the devil is in the details. Is anyone getting the details right? After reading about it, writing about it, and hearing about it all my working life, no one seems to be doing it.

This world is a big, big place. We're all world class at selling it. And last class at doing it.

Simple as that.

MACKAY'S MORAL

Believe me, there is a place in the world for any business
that takes care of its customers—after the sale.

Chapter 86

DISHING IT OUT

During the Depression movies were popular even though for many they were a luxury. Giveaways, like Dish Night and Bingo Night, helped boost attendance.

Human nature has not been repealed. Prizes and contests are still used to sell lots of things, from magazines to hamburgers.

So why not surveys? If you want to know what's on your customers' minds, doesn't it make sense to give them a reason to tell you?

The lodging industry spends a ton of money printing and distributing surveys and the national average return is a dismal 1 percent.

Why?

They don't give their customers any incentive to fill them out.

Millions of people sit in hotel rooms with nothing to do, and 99 percent of them practice their one-hand set shots by crumpling up their survey cards and tossing them at the wastebasket.

Is it any wonder why?

A hundred ridiculous questions. "How were your eggs?" (If they were cold or runny, you already told the waitress in the coffee shop.)

"Were there enough stationery and envelopes in the room?" (I always answer this one. There are never enough envelopes. Order more. Grosses and grosses of them.)

Teeny-weeny type.

Seven categories of questions: room, bathroom, food, service, desk, amenities . . . I can't remember the other, maybe it's another envelope question, but who wants to drag themselves back to their room after a four-hour flight and six hours of meetings and then take an MBA exam on soap or pillow chocolates?

Who's asking? Why? Who knows.

A while ago, I spoke to the staffs of the three Pointe Hilton Resorts in Phoenix and took my own survey:

"How many are filled out?" Same old question.

"About 1 percent." Same old answer.

"How would you like to double or triple that percentage?"

"Sure."

"Two little tweaks. One: you get 10 questions. Max. More than that is off-putting, and those that do fill out those 100-question beauties are mostly entertaining themselves by thinking up phony answers. Two: this is the biggie. At the top of the form, in big, bold, block letters: 'Win An All-Expense-Paid Three-Day Trip to the Super Bowl For Two . . . in One Minute.' "

"That's it?"

"That's it. If you want to PR it a bit, you can make a big deal out of the drawing, have a party and a celebrity to pull the winning card out of a giant fishbowl, that sort of thing. And you may not even have to pay for the plane tickets, if you promote the airline on the survey card and at the drawing."

Mackay's Moral

Question: What's the difference between winning a cereal bowl on Dish Night and winning a Super Bowl ticket? Answer: There isn't any. Motivate your customers with incentives and they'll do what you want them to do.

QUICKIES

Chapter 87

OLYMPIC CHAMPIONS RIDE THE PINE

Riding the pine, sitting the bench, carrying the water, call it what you will . . . it's all the same. It's the guy or gal who doesn't get put in the game until the score is so lopsided the C or D player couldn't possibly hurt anything.

Sometimes these are young players in training. They watch the pros with the "lean and hungry look" of Cassius in *Julius Caesar* and burn with impatience until they get their turn to shine.

But more often than not, these benchwarmers are players whose glory days mostly exist in the scrapbooks they pull out when fans or relatives show up at the house. Whether it's through injury, age, laziness, or lack of heart, they've lost the edge.

Or maybe they haven't lost it at all. Maybe they've just stayed the same while the superstars kept improving.

Think about your performance. How do you rate your current capabilities compared to 10 years ago? How about five years ago? One year ago?

If you're not making significant efforts to continually improve, you're not staying the same, you're falling behind. Why? Because your competition is continually raising the bar. Want some proof?

I was at the pool in Munich in 1972 when Mark Spitz dominated the Olympic swimming competition with an unheard-of seven gold medals. I was there again in Atlanta in 1996 where, even with his then-record-breaking times, Spitz would not have made the team.

At the 1980 Olympics Eric Heiden won five gold medals in speed skating. By the 1998 Olympics Heiden's fastest gold-medal-winning time would have put him in 40th place!

In 1994 Dan Jansen blew away the 1,000-meter speed skating competition at Lillehammer. Just four years later, in 1998, his times would have put him in 19th place!

MACKAY'S MORAL

Sharpen your edges. We can't always be the best . . .
but we can always be the best we can be.

Chapter 88

GETTING YOUR OWN COFFEE

E-mail and the other features of the electronic office revolution, together with restructurings and downsizings, have decimated the ranks of secretaries. At the same time, coffee shops have been perking up everywhere. What's the connection?

Secretaries used to tote coffee to their bosses every morning from the company coffee pot. Secretaryless middle managers now do their own fetch and carry, and smart marketers have found them to be an easy and inviting target for "gourmet" coffee. Fewer secretaries equals more coffee shops. Who would have guessed it?

Middle manager, meet your new secretary. No, not Ms. Starbucks or Mr. Caribou—your PC. It won't bring you coffee or laugh at your unfunny jokes, but if you learn to treat it right, it can perform a lot of the support functions your secretary once did.

MACKAY'S MORAL

Never underestimate the impact of the law of
unexpected consequences.

Chapter 89

WISDOM? YOU BET YOUR APHORISM!

When I was a kid, my dad, who was the AP correspondent in St. Paul, Minnesota, would take me down to his office. It was a wonderful place.

What made the biggest impression on me were the walls. They were covered with the memorabilia of a lifetime of front-row seats. They were his favorites from among the countless stories and columns he had written. There were the autographed photos and menus, fight posters, baseball tickets, convention schedules, political flyers, funeral programs, wedding invitations, all linked one to another by a series of his pet aphorisms. He had made up some of this fortune cookie wisdom himself. Some was straight from the cookie, printed on those tiny slips of paper and occasionally stained with tea.

As a result, I've been an aphorism junkie all my life.

I hang them on my own walls, carry them in my wallet, put them in my books, and stick them in my speeches.

Here are my favorites. Like my dad's, some are my own, others are of more uncertain ancestry.

- You can take any amount of pain as long as you know it's going to end.
- I know that you don't know . . . but you don't know that you don't know.

- It's not what you eat . . . it's what's eating you.
- While on the ladder of success, don't step back to admire your work.
- They don't pay off on effort . . . they pay off on results.
- Most people emphasize What should I buy? What should I sell? Wrong question. More appropriate is When should I buy? When should I sell?
- Those who have free seats hiss first.
- People begin to become successful the minute they decide to be.
- Good habits are as addictive as bad habits and a lot more rewarding.
- People always remember two things: who kicked you when you were down, and who helped you up.
- Putting your sales force on salary is like playing ball without keeping score: when nobody wins or loses, nobody cares.
- It never hurts to let the other person feel they're smarter than you.
- If you win say little. If you lose say less.
- If you want to triple your success ratio, you have to triple your failure rate.
- Your day usually goes the way the corners of your mouth turn.
- If you don't know where you are going, any road will get you there.
- A person wrapped up in himself makes a pretty small package.
- If you think education is expensive . . . try ignorance.
- He or she who rides a tiger can't dismount.
- When a person strikes in anger, he usually misses the mark.
- On the day of victory no one is tired.
- Compromise is always wrong when it means sacrificing principle.
- Cooperation can be spelled with two letters—WE.

- An old broom knows the dirty corners best.
- You will never get ahead of anyone as long as you are trying to get even with them.

MACKAY'S MORAL

Weren't those enough?

SEALING THE ENVELOPE

Chapter 90

LETTERS FOR LIVING

As an international speaker and writer, I receive literally thousands of letters and e-mails, many of which are from people suggesting I write about certain topics important to them.

One topic that is suggested frequently is praise. I've always said, "A pat on the back accomplishes more than a slap in the face."

Edward A. Maznio sent me this moving story about Sister Helen Mrosia that provides a great lesson about how we tend to be more negative than positive in our comments. We should encourage everyone to compliment others more often, especially the ones we love and care about. Nobody's attention ever wavers when someone pays them a compliment.

He was in the first third-grade class I taught at St. Mary's School in Morris, Minnesota. All 34 of my students were dear to me, but Mark Eklund was "one in a million." Very neat in appearance, but had that happy-to-be-alive attitude that made even his occasional mischievousness delightful.

Mark talked incessantly. I had to remind him again and again that talking without permission was not acceptable. What impressed me so much, though, was his sincere response every time I had to correct him for misbehaving. "Thank you for correcting me, Sister!" I didn't know what to make of it at first, but before long I became accustomed to hearing it many times a day.

One morning my patience was growing thin when Mark talked once too often, and then I made a novice teacher's mistake. I looked at him and said, "If you say one more word, I am going to tape your mouth shut!" It wasn't 10 seconds later when Chuck (another student) blurted out, "Mark is talking again."

I hadn't asked any of the students to help me watch Mark, but since I had stated the punishment in front of the class, I had to act on it. I remember the scene as if it had occurred this morning. I walked to my desk, very deliberately opened my drawer, and took out a roll of masking tape. Without saying a word, I proceeded to Mark's desk, tore off two pieces of tape, and made a big X with them over his mouth. I then returned to the front of the room. As I glanced at Mark to see how he was doing he winked at me.

That did it! I started laughing. The class cheered as I walked back to Mark's desk, removed the tape, and shrugged my shoulders. His first words were, "Thank you for correcting me, Sister."

At the end of the year I was asked to teach junior-high math. The years flew by, and before I knew it Mark was in my classroom again. He was more handsome than ever and just as polite. Since he had to listen carefully to my instructions in the "new math," he did not talk as much in ninth grade as he had in third.

One Friday things just didn't feel right. We had worked hard on a new concept all week, and I sensed that the students were frowning, frustrated with themselves, and edgy with one another. I had to stop this crankiness before it got out of hand. So I asked them to list the names of the other students in the room on two sheets of paper, leaving a space between each name.

Then I told them to think of the nicest thing they could say about each of their classmates and write it down. It took the remainder of the class period to finish the assignment, and as the students left the room, each one handed me the papers.

Mark said, "Thank you for teaching me, Sister. Have a good weekend."

That Saturday I wrote down the name of each student on a separate sheet of paper, and I listed what everyone else had said about that individual. On Monday I gave each student his or her list. Before long the entire class was smiling. "Really?" I heard whispered. "I never knew that meant anything to anyone!" "I didn't know others liked me so much!"

No one ever mentioned those papers in class again. I never knew if they discussed them after class or with their parents, but it didn't matter. The exercise had accomplished its purpose. The students were happy with themselves and one another again.

That group of students moved on. Several years later, after I returned from vacation, my parents met me at the airport. As we were driving home, mother asked me the usual questions about the trip . . . the weather, my experiences in general. There was a lull in the conversation. My father cleared his throat as he usually did before something important.

"The Eklunds called last night," he began.

"Really?" I said. "I haven't heard from them in years. I wonder how Mark is."

Dad responded quietly. "Mark was killed in Vietnam," he said. "The funeral is tomorrow, and his parents would like it if you could attend. . . ."

I had never seen a serviceman in a military coffin before. Mark looked so handsome, so mature. All I could think at that moment was, "Mark, I would give all the masking tape in the world if only you would talk to me."

The church was packed with Mark's friends. Chuck's sister sang "The Battle Hymn of the Republic." Why did it have to rain on the day of the funeral? It was difficult enough at the graveside. The pastor said the usual prayers, and the bugler played taps. One by one those who loved Mark took a last walk by the coffin and sprinkled it with holy water.

I was the last one to bless the coffin. As I stood there, one of the soldiers who had acted as a pallbearer came up to me. "Were you Mark's math teacher?" he asked. I nodded as I continued to stare at the coffin. "Mark talked about you a lot," he said.

After the funeral, Mark's father said, "We want to show you something," taking a wallet out of his pocket. "They found this on Mark when he was killed. We thought you might recognize it."

Opening the billfold, he carefully removed two worn pieces of notebook paper that had obviously been taped, folded, and refolded many times. I knew without looking that the papers were the ones on which I had listed all the good things each of Mark's classmates had said about him.

"Thank you so much for doing that," Mark's mother said. "As you can see, Mark treasured it."

Mark's classmates started to gather around us. Charlie smiled rather sheepishly and said, "I still have my list. It's in the top drawer of my desk at home."

Chuck's wife said, "Chuck asked me to put his in our wedding album."

"I have mine, too," Marilyn said. "It's in my diary."

Then Vicki, another classmate, reached into her pocketbook, took out her wallet, and showed her worn and frazzled list to the group. "I carry this with me at all times," Vicki said without batting an eyelash. "I think we all saved our lists."

That's when I finally sat down and cried. I cried for Mark and for all his friends who would never see him again.

What a beautiful testimonial to the impact a simple act of praise can have on the lives of others.

I had a similar experience in my own life.

Because my mother had died several months after my college graduation, and my sister was already married, my dad and I lived alone together for about three years. During those years we had many long and substantive talks. So much of what became my blueprint for living, including both business success and personal happiness, came out of those father-son bull sessions.

Fifteen years later, when my dad died very suddenly at the age of 69, I was not surprised to find a wonderful letter he'd written to my sister and me to be read after his death. After thanking us for helping to make his life such a complete, happy, and exciting one, he reminded us of some of the things he wanted us to remember in dealing with others.

He said not to forget *how important it is to compliment and praise others so we can never feel sorry for something left unsaid.* In addition, he stressed how one wrong act could erase a lifetime of good and moral behavior. *Even if you lose everything,* his letter went on, *you will always have your good name if you protect it well.*

I think often of those words, and in trying to pass on Jack Mackay's life lessons, I have endeavored to be the person he wanted me to become. Like the students in the earlier story, I keep that letter close to me and find myself reading it regularly as a reminder of how to live my life.

I hope his ideas, and my belief that you can do anything you put your mind to, will help you, too.

MACKAY'S MORAL

Nothing will improve a person's hearing more than sincere praise.

If you have thoughts, comments, or ideas about this book, I'd love to hear from you. (Please, no requests for personal advice.) Write to me at the following address:

Harvey Mackay
Mackay Envelope Corporation
2100 Elm Street Southeast
Minneapolis, MN 55414

I also can be reached electronically. My E-mail address is Harvey@Mackay.com
My Web Site address is http://www.mackay.com

Index

values 331–336
values, business 217–218
Veeck, Bill 305–306
Velveeta 239
Vernon, Lillian 29
VHS 168
volunteer work 41–43

Walgreen, Charles 49, 51
Walgreen's 49
Walker, Jimmy 111, 113
Wall Drug 29–30
Washington, George 257
Watergate 259
Webster, Noah 58
Webster's Dictionary 58
Welch, Jack 277–278

Wendmark, Bill 14
Wepner, Chuck 17
West Point 25
Westenberg, Bob 264
Whitehead, John C. 109
Williams, Ted 195
Wilson, Larry 229
winning 20–25
Wonder Bread 239
Woods, Tiger 291
Wright Brothers 58

Xerox 18, 266

zero tolerance, selective use of 199
Zigler, Zig 163

ABOUT THE AUTHOR

HARVEY MACKAY is chief executive officer of the $85 million Mackay Envelope Corporation, a business he founded in 1959 in Minneapolis. In addition, he is a nationally syndicated weekly business columnist, #1 *New York Times* bestselling author, and internationally acclaimed speaker. He and his wife of thirty-eight years, Carol Ann, have three children and five grandchildren, and live in a suburb of Minneapolis.